As one of the world's longest established and best-known travel brands, Thomas Cook are the experts in travel.

For more than 135 years our guidebooks have unlocked the secrets of destinations around the world, sharing with travellers a wealth of experience and a passion for travel.

Rely on Thomas Cook as your travelling companion on your next tri and benefit from our unique heritag

D0533354

Thomas Cook **traveller** guides

CARIBBEAN CRUISING
Emma Stanford

Your travelling companion since 1873

Written by Emma Stanford, updated by Polly Thomas

Published by Thomas Cook Publishing
A division of Thomas Cook Tour Operations Limited.
Company registration no. 3772199 England
The Thomas Cook Business Park, Unit 9, Coningsby Road,
Peterborough PE3 8SB, United Kingdom
Email: books@thomascook.com, Tel: + 44 (0) 1733 416477
www.thomascookpublishing.com

Produced by Cambridge Publishing Management Limited
Burr Elm Court, Main Street, Caldecote CB23 7NU

ISBN: 978-1-84848-211-1

© 2003, 2006, 2008 Thomas Cook Publishing
This fourth edition © 2009
Text © Thomas Cook Publishing
Maps © Thomas Cook Publishing/PCGraphics (UK) Limited

Series Editor: Maisie Fitzpatrick
Production/DTP: Steven Collins

Printed and bound in Italy by Printer Trento

Cover photography: © Amy Strycula/Alamy

Contents

Introduction

Since 1492, when Christopher Columbus set sail in search of a western route to the spice islands of the East Indies, travellers have been captivated by the Caribbean. While Columbus signally failed to locate any spices, save pepper, he did discover a chain of gorgeous tropical islands with their spectacular white-sand beaches lapped by warm, translucent seas. Five hundred years later, the palm trees still sway in the trade winds and the sun shines throughout the year – an intoxicating blend for visitors from colder climes.

The majority of Caribbean cruises begin from the world's two busiest cruise-ship terminals in Florida (a holiday hotspot in its own right): the Port of Miami, and Port Everglades in Fort Lauderdale. And there can be no doubt that in the region cruising is the ultimate form of travel. Liberated from transport and luggage hassles or dining dilemmas, cruise passengers can truly relax and enjoy their vacation.

For some this may extend no further than enjoying a tall glass of Planter's Punch and a good book while on the pool deck. But part of the fun of Caribbean cruising is the variety of destinations visited in a short period of time. You'll wake up each morning with a new group of islands on the horizon, and a different port at the foot of the gangplank and, best of all, somebody else has done all the hard work to get you there.

Every island has its own special flavour. Colonial history may be

WHERE TO GO

This guide does not attempt to cover every island in the Caribbean region, or even every corner of the islands listed, as more remote spots are usually inaccessible to cruise passengers with limited time. However, in addition to sections devoted to the main Caribbean cruise embarkation ports of Miami and Fort Lauderdale, you'll find entries covering the top cruise-ship ports of call and accessible local attractions on more than 30 Caribbean islands, plus Bermuda, a summer season favourite in the Atlantic Ocean, and Key West, a US mainland stop on several cruise routes.

revealed in architecture, as in the toy-town Dutch gables of Curaçao, or there may be distinctive culinary influences such as the rotis of Trinidad and French-Creole dishes of Martinique. There's an island to suit all tastes and budgets, from super-chic St Barts to mellow Grenada, the elegant plantation hotels of Nevis to the lively Sunday sunset steel band sessions atop Shirley Heights in Antigua. Every island has its fair share of beaches, too, from the pink sands of the Bahamas or the pure white swathes of St Thomas and St John to the dramatic black-sand beaches of Dominica and St Vincent. And, at the end of the day, sightseers and sunseekers alike can enjoy the sunset fanned by a cooling breeze as the ship glides out of port, and partake of a gourmet dinner and a spot of entertainment before a stroll on the deck beneath impossibly starry skies.

'Every one of the islands has, for me, its own special scent . . . islands like Grenada or St Vincent float in a subtle aroma of spices.'
DANE CHANDOS
Isles to Windward, 1955

'The West Indies I behold
Like the Hesperides of old –
Trees of life with fruits of gold.'
JAMES MONTGOMERY
A Voyage Around the World, 1841

Glorious technicolour sunsets are a Caribbean speciality

The Caribbean

Collectively known as the Antilles, the Caribbean comprises more than 7,000 islands, which range in size from Cuba to tiny coral atolls just peeking above sea level. They begin, too, with Cuba, 144km (90 miles) off Key West and stretch south in an arc almost 4,023km (2,500 miles) long to the Lesser Antilles (Virgin Islands to Trinidad) in the south towards the South American coast at Venezuela.

To the north of the chain, the flat, swampy Florida peninsula has a porous limestone base that was formed by massive deposits of sediment packed in deep trenches between extinct underwater volcanoes. The Bermuda archipelago, over 1,600km (1,000 miles) out into the Atlantic Ocean, also has limestone underpinnings, and can claim the world's most northerly coral reefs, thanks to the warm waters of the Gulf Stream. To the south and east of Florida, meanwhile, the dozens of islands and tiny cays (small flat islets, pronounced 'keys') which make up the Bahamas Islands reach down towards

The Pitons du Carbet rise above Fort-de-France, Martinique

Boats in the Grenadine Islands

the Caribbean chain, which itself sits atop a rift between the Atlantic and Caribbean tectonic plates. It's this precarious position that caused the volcanic eruptions which created many of the islands, pushing them up out of the sea; some emerged from the ocean 20 to 30 million years ago. Nowhere are the Caribbean's volcanic origins more obvious than in the imposing, jungle-clad volcanic cones of the Windward Islands, of which St Lucia's Pitons are the most iconic example. Several Windward volcanoes are still active, and you can see (and smell) steaming, sulphurous volcanic activity in Dominica, St Lucia, Guadeloupe, Martinique and St Vincent, while the black sand beaches here are the result of age-old eruptions. To the north of the chain, meanwhile, many of the islands are ringed by coral reefs that, over the years, have created the brilliant white sand that the region is famed for, while these islands' limestone base has provided numerous dramatic cave networks, many of which have been opened up as visitor attractions.

Scenery varies dramatically from island to island. The mountainous uplands of Jamaica or Puerto Rico couldn't be a greater contrast to the low-lying limestone and coral Cayman Islands, or the Dutch Leewards with their spaghetti Western-style cacti and tortured-looking, windblown divi-divi trees. Conditions also differ between the windward (Atlantic) and leeward (Caribbean) sides of the islands. While the rocky coastline of the former is pounded by Atlantic rollers, the sandy strands of the latter are lapped by gentle waves and protected by offshore reefs that offer some fantastic snorkelling and diving, with brightly coloured sponges and anemones contrasting with corrugated brain corals, stands of rutted elkhorn coral and soft sea fans waving gently in the currents; the fish, meanwhile, come in every colour and size, from the yellow-, black- and white-striped sergeant major to the multihued parrot, leering eels and toothy barracudas. One thing the islands do have in common, however, is a dense tangle of interior rainforest that harbours a veritable treasury of plant and animal life – just 10sq km (4sq miles) can contain up to 750 species of trees, 1,000-plus varieties of smaller flowering plants, 400 species of birds, 125 types of mammal and 150 different butterflies and moths. Though European settlers cleared vast tracts for their plantations, leaving flatter islands such as Antigua virtually bare, mountainous islands such as Jamaica and Puerto Rico were more fortunate, their inaccessible uplands proving more than a match for the sugar barons. Other islands, such as Tobago and Guadeloupe, have designated large tracts of forest as protected reserves. Below the rainforest's canopy of mahogany, gommier and other massive trees, lianas (climbing plants) scramble up towards the light, and the vast greenery is festooned with ferns, mosses, orchids and bromeliads growing out of tree trunks and branches. The forest provides rich pickings for birdwatchers, with a host of colourful species, from toucans and parrots to bejewelled hummingbirds flitting through the trees.

Verdant vegetation in Guadeloupe

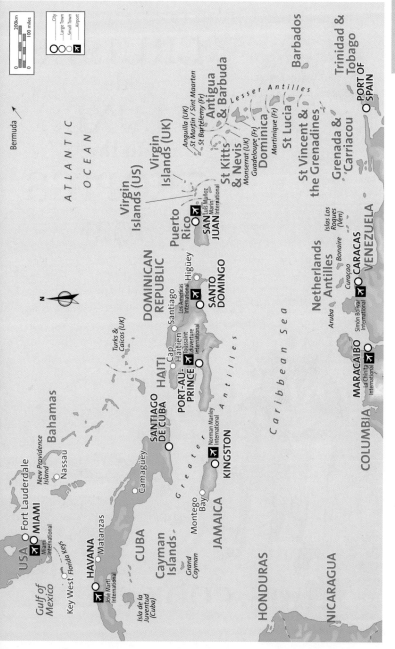

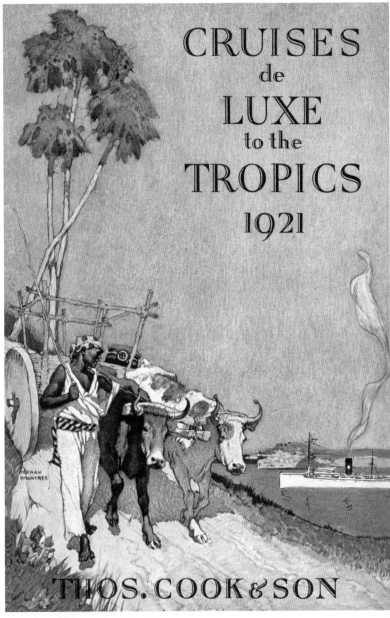

A vintage 1920s poster advertising cruises

On a less positive note, one other thing that the islands share is a deeply fragmented political scene, which has done nothing to assist the region's overall economic and social situation. Over the years, several attempts at providing the framework for a united front have dissolved into unseemly squabbles as the various participants seek to preserve the identity and interests of their individual nations – and of the outside interests which retain heavy influence in the region. In the 1950s and 1960s, when the Caribbean islands began to break free of their colonial shackles, the majority opted for full independence, but exceptions include the Crown Colonies of the British Virgin Islands, Cayman Islands, Bermuda, the Netherlands Antilles (though not Aruba, which is autonomous), and the French islands of Martinique and Guadeloupe, which are overseas Territories of France. The United States also wields considerable influence in the region; the USVI (St Thomas, St Croix and St John) are an unincorporated Territory of the USA with a self-elected Senate and Governor, and non-voting delegate to the US House of Representatives. Puerto Rico, meanwhile, is a Commonwealth of the USA, linked to the federal banking system and with an American-style government model. One issue dominates current Puerto Rican politics: whether the island remains a Commonwealth, or opts for statehood.

Established in the wake of the ill-fated West Indies Federation and CARIFTA (Caribbean Free Trade Association) CARICOM (the Caribbean Common Market) was set up in 1973 as a means of promoting economic integration in the region, fostering and developing trade and coordinating economic foreign policy. Though some initiatives have been successful, and CARICOM has endured over the years, the Caribbean is a long way from functioning as a thriving unified entity, with the region's farmers still reeling from the WTO's removal of preferential tariffs to EU markets. The region's main economic earner, however, is tourism. Though visitors holidaying in the resorts make the greatest contribution to the economy, CARICOM long had its eye on the cruise-ship industry, which was initially seen as a threat to the all-important stayover tourist trade. CARICOM's response was to levy higher taxes on cruise ships, but this didn't give any meaningful boost to the region's resorts; and in any case, the post-9/11 landscape means the region is heavily dependent on the huge amount of revenue that cruise ships bring to the Caribbean. In 2008, for example, the total cruise passenger arrivals for all the islands in the region numbered 14.4 million. And, with the world's finances looking rocky, the ports of call are doing all they can to make sure cruisers choose the Caribbean over other classic cruising routes.

History

1000 BC	First Amerindian tribes, the Ciboney, move to the Caribbean islands from South America.
AD 120	Peaceable Arawak Indians arrive from South America.
800	Warlike Carib Indians begin to push the Arawaks from the Lesser Antilles.
1492	12 October: Columbus makes landfall in the Bahamas at San Salvador.
1513	Juan Ponce de León steps ashore in Florida, and names the land after the date of his arrival, La Florida, the Spanish Eastertide Feast of Flowers.
1600s	'Golden Age' of Caribbean piracy with looting on the high seas.
1627	The English settle Barbados.
1655	The English seize Jamaica from Spain.
1814–15	West Indies carved up following the Treaties of Paris at the end of the Napoleonic Wars.
1834	The Emancipation Act abolishes slavery in Britain and its colonies.
1902	Mont Pelée erupts in Martinique and destroys the town of St-Pierre with 30,000 casualties.
1917	The USA purchases the Virgin Islands of St Croix, St John, and St Thomas from Denmark for $25 million.
1959	Revolution in Cuba led by Fidel Castro and Ernesto 'Che' Guevara. Castro is elected Prime Minister. Mass exodus of refugees to Miami.
1962	The Cuban Missile Crisis – attempts by the USSR to station nuclear missiles in Cuba are challenged by President John F Kennedy. The Russians back down.
1966	Barbados achieves independence from Britain.
1971	Walt Disney World® opens in Orlando with the Magic Kingdom®, followed by the EPCOT® Center (1983)

and Disney's Hollywood™ Studios (1989).

1974 Grenada gains independence.

1978 Dominica gains independence.

1979 St Lucia, St Vincent and the Grenadines become independent states.

1981 Antigua and Barbuda gain independence.

1983 St Kitts and Nevis become independent. A US–Eastern Caribbean force invades Grenada to end the socialist regime.

1993 Puerto Rico votes against US statehood, but for association with the USA, as an unincorporated territory.

1994 A US 'friendly' invasion reinstates Haiti's deposed President Aristide, but he is voted out in 1995.

1995 Hurricane Luis causes considerable damage in St Martin/Sint Maarten and other islands of the Caribbean.

1997 Montserrat's Soufrière volcano erupts, destroying the capital, Plymouth.

1998 Nevis fails in bid to separate from St Kitts.

2001 Trinidad-born V S Naipaul wins Nobel Prize for Literature.

2005 Florida and the Caribbean are ravaged by a record number of tropical storms and hurricanes.

2007 The Caribbean hosts the ICC Cricket World Cup.

2008 Fidel Castro resigns as Cuba's President in favour of his brother Raúl after nearly 50 years as the nation's leader.

2009 Trinidad hosts the fifth Summit of the Americas, with guest leaders including Barack Obama. Barbuda's Prime Minister Baldwyn Spencer renames Antigua's highest peak Mount Obama in honour of the newly inaugurated President of the United States.

Slavery

The first black African ever to set eyes on the Caribbean was Pedro Alonzo Niño. He was not a slave, but the navigator aboard the caravel *Niña*, one of three ships Columbus took on his first voyage to the New World. The slave trade between West Africa and Europe was established by this time and was, in fact, inspired by the Africans themselves. Domestic slavery of captured enemies was an accepted practice among African tribes, and they, in turn, sold their slaves to the Europeans in exchange for manufactured goods such as textiles, glass and weapons.

Heb. 3. 13.

PHŒBE.

Jamaica Royal Gazette, Oct. 7, 1826.

35—42   Spanish-Town Workhouse.

Notice is hereby given, that unless the undermentioned Slave is taken out of this Workhouse, prior to Monday the 30th day of October next, she will on that day, between the hours of 10 and 12 o'Clock in the forenoon, be put up to Public Sale, and sold to the highest and best bidder, at the Cross-Keys Tavern, in this Town, agreeably to the Workhouse Law now in force, for payment of her fees.

PHŒBE, a Creole, 5 feet 4½ inches, marked NELSON on breasts, and I O on right shoulder, first said to one Miss Roberts, a free Black, in Vere, secondly, to Thomas Oliver, Esq. St. John's, but it is very lately ascertained that her right name is Quasheba, and she belongs to Salisbury-Plain plantation, in St. Andrew's; Mr. John Smith is proprietor.   May 11

Ordered, that the above be published in the Newspapers appointed by Law, for Eight Weeks.

By order of the Commissioners,

T. RENNALLS, Sup.

" To admit Slave-evidence (of course cautiously and properly guarded) and to abolish the stripping of women, are two desirable points, and would destroy topics used with much effect against the Colonies."

Letter of J. R. Gronell, Esq. (a West India Proprietor,) to the Editor of the Jamaica Journal and Kingston Chronicle, August 1, 1826.

A notice of a slave sale

As South America and the West Indies were colonised and the native Amerindian population (the very first Caribbean slaves) were decimated by disease and ill-treatment, the search began for a replacement workforce to dig gold mines and tend the tobacco and sugar plantations.

The result was the infamous 'triangular trade' which took slavery to a level of unimaginable atrocity. Manufactured goods were shipped from Europe to be exchanged for West African slaves. The human cargo was then transported in appalling conditions on the notorious middle passage to the New World where the ships were loaded with raw materials – sugar, spices, cotton, tobacco and rum – for Europe. It has been estimated that during the 250-year heyday of the Caribbean slave trade, as many as 40 million Africans were transported to the West Indies, the largest forced transportation of human beings in history. One in eight died on the middle passage.

Conditions were little better for the survivors on arrival. Sold at auctions like animals, slaves were then 'seasoned' with strict discipline. Beatings, brandings and the frequent use of neck chains, leg irons and other torturous devices were common. To further break their spirit and ties to African culture, families were split up and slaves were forbidden to speak in their native tongue. They worked 18-hour days, and children as young as five were put to work weeding and picking cane. Contemporary records show that up to 30 per cent of the slave population died every four years.

It was economics, not morals, that finally put paid to the slave trade. There were heroic abolitionists without doubt – Granville Sharp, Thomas Clarkson and William Wilberforce in Britain, and Victor Schoelcher in France, among them.

But the introduction of sugar beet in Europe made the colonial trade less viable, and in 1838 (four years after the Emancipation Act) abolition finally became a reality in Britain. France followed suit in 1848.

Two excellent museums that explore the slave trade and the horrors of the middle passage are the Museum Kura Hulanda in Curaçao (*see p109*) and the African Heritage Museum in San Juan, Puerto Rico (*see p112*). The first displays a life-size reconstruction of a slave ship that once sailed from the African coast. Other artefacts include musical instruments, sculptures and wooden masks.

Contemporary paintings presented a stylised (and sanitised) view of slavery

Culture

Like the product of any great melting pot, Caribbean culture is the sum of its ingredients and the recipe, in this case, is deliciously exotic. Take a pinch of Spanish influence, a generous measure of French élan and British reserve, add a peck of Dutch and Danish, a dash of Portuguese and American, then season generously with West African rhythm and Indian spice – et voilà!

Architecture

A hybrid to the core, Caribbean architecture is both varied and colourful. As a rule, the islands' colonial rulers imported techniques from the home country and adapted them to suit the heat.

So, for example, you'll find the sturdy stone Georgian buildings of ex-British St Kitts and Antigua adorned with louvred shutters and shady balconies. There is a wealth of pretty fretwork decoration too. Commonly known as 'gingerbread', these carved wooden frills and curlicues adorn porches, gables and eaves right around the West Indies; they're also popular in Key West where they were introduced by the Bahamanian migrants around the turn of the 20th century.

In some cases, bits of the 'old country' were simply transplanted wholesale to the New World, such as the cobbled streets of Puerto Rico's Old San Juan.

Language

English is the unofficial language of the tourist industry throughout the Caribbean, though this might not help much in the French (and resolutely Francophile) islands of Guadeloupe and Martinique. Although French is also the official language of St Barts and St Martin, English is understood; similarly, Spanish is the first language of Puerto Rico, but English is also widely spoken. The everyday language used by the islanders is patois, which may seem comprehensible at first (particularly if you speak some French), but then dissolves into something incomprehensible the minute you think you understand. The most common form of patois is Creole, a mixture of French, Portuguese and West African laced with occasional English words; in St Lucia and some other islands in the Lesser Antilles, *kweyol*, as it's called, is a distinct language, with unique rules of grammar and syntax.

Music

Music is the heartbeat of the Caribbean. From Trinidadian calypso and soca to Jamaican reggae, you will find its infectious rhythms are as much a part of the Caribbean experience as palm trees and Planter's Punch. If you get the chance to attend any of the region's carnivals – do not miss out – *see pp20–21* for more on Carnival.

You'll find live music shows in all of the resorts, and cruise ship passengers are often serenaded by mento or steel pan bands as they disembark, while after dark, DJs spin the latest reggae and soca hits at the region's many regular outdoor 'jump-ups'.

Religion

Since the earliest European settlers arrived, Christianity has been the official religion of the Caribbean, and many of the oldest surviving buildings are churches. As a rough guide, the former Spanish and French islands are Roman Catholic; the numerous old churches on British islands are generally Protestant with a high quota of Baptist and Methodist worshippers.

Rastafarianism has spread from Jamaica, where it first appeared in the 1930s as an offshoot of the peaceful black pride movement. Turning away from Western culture, young West Indians looked to their African roots for a new religious and cultural identity. True Rastas are God-fearing types, both vegetarian and teetotal. Cultural identity is expressed through reggae music, the use of ganja (marijuana) to gain spiritual wisdom and the sporting of dreadlocks to represent the natural glory of the lion's mane (one title of their former spiritual leader, Emperor Haile Selassie of Ethiopia, was the 'Conquering Lion of Judah').

Caribbean folklore

Though Caribbean societies are generally pretty modern in outlook, you may well notice a superstitious streak in people throughout the islands. Though most folk dismiss talk of ghosts and ghouls, the tales' ghostly characters – known variously as duppies or jumbies – do survive, first brought to the region with slaves from West Africa and adapted over the years into a uniquely Caribbean form. One of the most common of the beings said to haunt lonely roads at night is the douen, a malevolent child spirit with feet that face backwards and a featureless face. Female temptresses abound, too, from the River Mumma or Mama L'Eau, a beautiful woman who lurks in forest pools and draws hapless young men to a watery death. Of the male characters, Papa Bois is the guardian of the forest, a tall figure with hair entwined by leaves who imitates animal calls in order to lure hunters deep into the bush.

Festivals and events

You're never far from a party in the Caribbean, with everything from carnivals and raucous New Year celebrations to world-class music festivals. On the sporting front, the region also hosts some top-class events, from golf competitions to regattas. The list below represents the best of the bunch. Note that things slow down considerably during the wet months of the hurricane season. For a comprehensive listing of all events in the region, check out the events calendar at www.onecaribbean.org

January
Carnival, Curaçao and Aruba
A series of competitions and parties that culminate in a street parade; festivities last for seven weeks in Curaçao, a month in Aruba.
Curaçao. Tel: (5999) 461 3352; www.curacaocarnival.info. Aruba. Tel: (297) 582 3777; www.aruba.com

Air Jamaica Jazz and Blues Festival, Montego Bay, Jamaica
A world-class music festival that attracts the cream of jazz and R&B acts from the O'Jays to Lionel Richie and Estelle.
Tel: (876) 383 8110; www.jamaicajazzandblues.com

February/March
Carnival, Trinidad and Tobago, Dominica, Bonaire, Grenada, St Barts
Trinidad and Tobago hosts the biggest and best of all the Caribbean carnivals, while the other events are more modest and intimate, but still lots of fun. All are pre-Lenten celebrations, so dates change annually.
Dominica: www.dominicacarnival.com
Trinidad & Tobago: www.visittnt.com
Bonaire: www.tourismbonaire.com
Grenada: www.grenadagrenadines.com
St Barts: www.st-barths.com

March
Heineken Regatta, St Maarten/ St Martin
The largest regatta in the Caribbean with lots of action at sea and huge parties on shore.
Tel: (973) 627 8180; www.heinekenregatta.com

Holders Season, Barbados
Prestigious cultural event, with two weeks of classical concerts, theatre and opera.
Tel: (246) 432 6385; www.holders.net

April
Carnival, US Virgin Islands
A week-long round of parades and music.

Tel: (340) 690 5552;
www.vicarnival.com

Buccoo Goat Races, Tobago
Part party, part serious competition, with goats and their trainers racing along the tracks all day.
Tel: (868) 639 2125;
www.visittobago.gov.tt

Sir Garfield Sobers Festival of Golf, Barbados
Four-day tournament that attracts players from all over the world.
Tel: (246) 428 8463;
www.barbadosgolfclub.com

Antigua Sailing Week
One of the biggest and best regattas in the world with six days of racing, competitions and fantastic parties.
Tel: (268) 462 8872;
www.sailingweek.com

May

Cayman Carnival Batabano, Grand Cayman
Four days of music, dancing and street parades in George Town.
Tel: (324) 949 7121;
www.caymancarnival.com

St Lucia Jazz Festival
The biggest and best of the region's jazz festivals with a host of local and international acts performing at Pigeon Island National Park.
Tel: (758) 452 4094;
www.stluciajazz.org

June

Vincy Mas, St Vincent
Week-long carnival in St Vincent with a host of calypso street parades and competitions.
Tel: (784) 457 2580;
www.carnivalsvg.com

July

Crop Over, Barbados and Carnival, St Lucia
Barbados' carnival is one of the biggest in the region, with a month of parties and competitions and a huge costume parade in August. St Lucia's celebration is a lot smaller.
Barbados: Tel: (246) 427 2623;
www.ncf.bb
St Lucia: Tel: (758) 452 1859.
www.luciancarnival.com

August

Antigua Carnival, Grenada Carnival
Parties and two days of soca and calypso parades in St John and St George's.
Antigua: Tel: (268) 463 9522;
www.antigua-barbuda.org
Grenada: Tel: (473) 440 0621;
www.spicemasgrenada.com

December

Junkanoo, Bahamas
Huge street parades – 'rushes' – on Boxing Day and January 1st, with costumes and music played on drums, conch shells and cowbells.
Tel: (242) 324 1714;
www.junkanoo.com

Carnival

The explosion of colour, music, singing and dance that is the Caribbean carnival actually has its roots in medieval Europe. The very word 'carnival' is derived from the Italian carnevale, which means the removal of meat, and refers to the Christian practice of Lenten abstinence in the period before Easter. The Europeans brought carnival to the New World, notably the Spanish and the French Catholic planters who

Costumes are essential ingredients of the carnival scene…

decamped to Trinidad as revolutionary unrest hit the French possessions at the end of the 18th century.

Between Christmas and Ash Wednesday, the French settlers indulged in a hectic season of parties and masked balls or masquerades, which, shortened to 'Mas', is still a commonly used Trinidadian term for the street parades of costume bands during carnival. With Emancipation in 1834, and the lifting of laws prohibiting slave gatherings and drumming, the former slaves celebrated their freedom every August with processions, took to the streets for fun at Christmas, and before long, hijacked the pre-Lenten Mardi Gras. The result was a fusion of West African and European traditions where folklore performances partnered stilt-riding moko-jumbies (make-believe spirits) with characters straight out of biblical tales, and stately quadrilles or waltzes were revamped to an African beat. The emergence of calypso in the 19th century and steel bands in the 1940s (*see p135*) set a truly Caribbean seal on the event. Today, costumed bands of thousands of revellers dance through the streets to the strains of soca music pumped from speaker-laden trucks.

Trinidad is still the home of Caribbean carnival (*see p132*), but

... and are often elaborate and colourful

every island has its own version. Some, like Bahamanian Junkanoo, are held over the Christmas period, while July and August see the Crop Over (harvest) and Emancipation carnivals on many islands, with the celebration in Barbados being the biggest.

Highlights

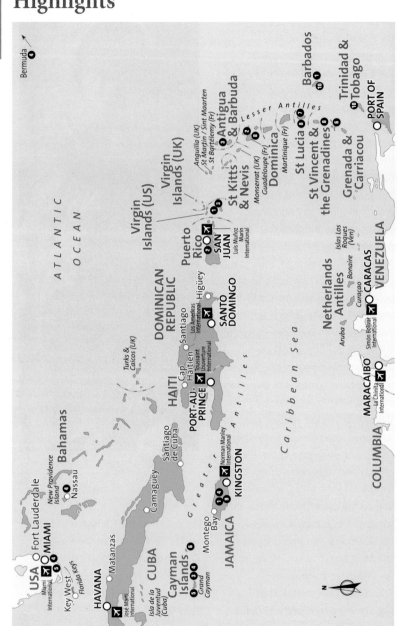

1 Golf Montego Bay's three seaside courses make Jamaica a golfer's paradise, while Mahogany Run in St Thomas is one of the region's most scenic courses, and Barbados' Sandy Lane the most prestigious. (*See pp181, 184 & 188.*)

2 Rainforest hikes From a trek around Puerto Rico's El Yunque to Guadeloupe's Parc Naturel, the Caribbean's rainforests offer a cool and fascinating alternative to the beach. (*See pp91–2 & 113.*)

3 Beaches Trunk Bay, St John's US Virgin Islands, Seven Mile Beach in Grand Cayman and all 365 of Antigua's pristine shorelines are just some of the Caribbean's spectacular beaches. (*See pp50, 74 & 141–2.*)

4 Dolphin and stingray encounters Getting up close and personal with friendly bottlenose dolphins or handfeeding graceful stingrays is a truly magical experience; take the plunge in Jamaica, Grand Cayman, Miami, Nassau and Bermuda. (*See pp38–9, 59, 71 & 75.*)

5 Shopping From a carved calabash shell, a bottle of pepper sauce or fine aged rum to a duty-free designer watch or handbag, the Caribbean's shops and craft markets offer some truly rich pickings. (*See p156–9.*)

6 Snorkelling and scuba diving The Caribbean boasts some truly spectacular sites, with the Cayman Islands, Bonaire, St Lucia and the Grenadine islands of St Vincent offering some of the richest pickings. (*See p160.*)

7 Soft adventure Many Caribbean islands offer exciting activities to get your adrenaline pumping, from swinging along a zipline in the rainforest canopy to tubing along rushing rivers or even trying your hand on a bobsleigh run. (*See p163.*)

8 Volcanic scenery Rising sharply out of the water on the southeast coast, St Lucia's Pitons are easily the Caribbean's most scenic volcanic peaks, but you can also climb volcanoes in Guadeloupe and St Vincent. (*See pp91–2, 122 & 127.*)

9 Creole food Fresh from the ocean, seafood is cooked to perfection throughout the Caribbean, while the spicy, smoky flavour of Jamaican jerk chicken or the clean tang of Bahamian conch salad are memorable highlights of local food. (*See p148–51.*)

10 Festivals Vibrant carnivals, exciting Junkanoo 'rushes' and world-class music festivals are just some of the annual round of special events in the Caribbean festival calendar. (*See pp18–19.*)

Cruising routes

With such a huge amount of choice on offer, picking the Caribbean cruise that's right for you can be a baffling experience. Do you go for a themed jaunt aboard a Disney megaship, a sophisticated trip on a small-scale luxury line or choose the middle ground and join the masses on a mainstream cruise?

The key is to think carefully about what you really want from your holiday, and to do as much research as you can before you commit – after all, there's no turning back once you're on board, so getting it right is crucial. Do you want to party every night with like-minded fellow cruisers, with the option to grab a snack from the 24-hour cafeteria, or would you prefer a gourmet dinner followed by a game of cards? Do you have a young family that will need to be entertained, or would you prefer to set sail on an adults-only ship? Another possibility to consider is going on a themed cruise, in which you set sail with a group of like-minded people. In the Caribbean, themed cruises vary greatly. Offerings from luxury lines such as Silversea might range from 'enrichment' cruises with on-board lectures on Caribbean history and culture and suitably erudite shore excursions, to itineraries planned around the region's golf courses. Carnival offers more mainstream

themes, from a Jimmy Buffet Tribute Cruise to a Single Parents' trip.

All of the main cruise lines have websites that can give you an idea of their flavour and target market, as well as their upcoming itineraries of themed cruises, but a good way to start your research is by looking at a specialist guide book such as *Fodor's Complete Guide to Caribbean Cruising*, which gives the lowdown of all the lines, from cabin size to dining to on-ship amenities. Another good bet is the *Berlitz Complete Guide to Cruising and Cruise Ships*, which includes some good money-saving tips as well as breaking down the cruise lines by market classification. The Internet is also a good resource with sites such as *www.cruisecritic.co.uk*, *www.cruise.co.uk*, *www.reviewthatcruise.com*, *www.cruisemates.com* and *www.cruisediva.com* providing a wealth of information as well as no-holds-barred reviews from passengers. Additionally, travel agents affiliated to CLIA (Cruise Lines International

Association) and ACE (Association of Cruise Experts) have specialist knowledge of the cruise market. There are also cruise agents who deal exclusively in cruise holidays, and they are often a good source of special deals and last-minute discounts.

Choosing a cruise

Just as today's cruise passengers are a diverse crowd, so are the cruising options that await them, and the mainstream cruise ships pride themselves on catering to a broad band of customers. They promise excellent food, modern facilities, a wide range of general activities and evening entertainment. Most incorporate some form of children's programme, too, particularly in the school holidays, from entertainment to childcare for babies, toddlers and older kids. One of the key things to think about when choosing your ideal ship, however, is facilities. The huge mega-boats will have far more on-board amenities – Royal Caribbean's brand new *Oasis of the Seas*, weighing in at 220,000 tons and with capacity for 5,400 passengers, is longer than a football field, and has everything from ziplines from the atrium to the decks, three pools (and ten whirlpools), as well as climbing walls, a spa and more restaurants and bars than you can count on both hands. Smaller ships, however, have the advantage of offering more personalised service, and while you might not have a pool or a wraparound

deck with a jogging track, there could be the possibility of taking a swim from a specialised watersports platform, and you'll be sharing the on-board space (and ports of call) with far fewer fellow passengers. Of course, the biggest difference between the mainstream fleets and the smaller, more specialised lines is price; the cost of a Caribbean cruise on the upscale Star Clippers, Windstar, Cunard, Seabourne, Sundream or Silversea lines might be three or four times more than the price of a similar itinerary with one of the mainstream lines such as Royal Caribbean, Carnival, Holland America, Princess or Celebrity. Another factor to

The Bahamas are well geared for tourism

consider when it comes to pricing is season; travel in the peak of the Caribbean tourist season (December to April), and you're likely to pay a premium; opt to cruise during the latter part of the hurricane season (Sept and Oct) and you may get substantial discounts. Other ways to get reductions on the brochure prices of cruises are the websites listed above, which often have deals, and to book well in advance to take advantage of special offers, or late enough to mop up unsold cabins, which are often discounted. But, however you book, always shop around first. Other factors which can reduce or bump up the cost of your cruise include your choice of cabin – on many ships, the layout and furnishings of cabins are pretty standard, but the price goes up in relation to convenience of location. As you probably won't spend a huge amount of time in your cabin, given all the on-ship activities and shore excursions, you may well be happy to have a less favourable position. On the other hand, if a state room with a private outdoor patio is essential to you, bear in mind that you will pay handsomely for it. It also pays to check exactly what is included in the price. All meals are usually part of the package, but drinks are not – and this may extend as far as the bottle of water on your dinner table, the espresso to finish your meal and the frothy welcome drink that you're handed when you board. Remember also that you'll need

to budget for additional expenses such as shore excursions, bar bills, laundry, in-room movies, yoga or pilates classes, spa treatments and staff tips at the end of the cruise (*see p177*), and remember that you'll also have to shell out for airfares to get you to your departure port. Most cruise lines can arrange flights for you, but it's well worth checking whether you can get a better deal independently.

Itineraries

As to itineraries, most Caribbean cruises last for seven nights and dock at between four and seven islands, but you can also get three- or four-night trips, and ten- or fourteen-night trips that take in Mexico and head down the Panama Canal. As a rule, short cruises are more popular with the younger end of the market. Cruises lasting ten days or more tend to charge a significantly higher rate per day, and the average age of the passengers rises accordingly. The majority of Caribbean cruises are round-trips, departing from and returning to the same port. Most depart from Miami or Fort Lauderdale, but those that start out at Puerto Rico can pack in up to six destinations in just a week. The downside to Puerto Rico departures is less flexibility in terms of flight availability and less competitive pricing on airfares when compared to flights to Florida. And, in terms of routes, the size of your ship will also determine where your ship docks. The huge mega-ships often favour larger

Cruise ship anchored at Charlotte Amalie, St Thomas

islands with roomy, state-of-the-art cruise ship terminals, while smaller vessels can put in at more remote places that many ships don't visit – although bear in mind that large ships can dock offshore without a designated terminal, and transport passengers to land in small boats known as tenders, which is a lot more time-consuming than simply stepping onto the dock.

Cruise ship operators usually divide the Caribbean into regions. In Eastern Caribbean itineraries, the big ships of mainstream lines departing from Florida ports may stop at San Juan in Puerto Rico, the US Virgin Islands (usually St Thomas) and St Maarten/ St Martin, as well as a visit to their 'private' islands in the Bahamian chain. Smaller ships may also dock at Tortola

in the British Virgin Islands and St Barts. Western Caribbean itineraries leaving Florida usually mean stops at Key West, Grand Cayman, Jamaica (Montego Bay and Ocho Rios), all hugely busy and very commercialized ports; longer trips might extend down to Cozumel on the Mexican Yucatán Caribbean coast, or even Belize City and the Bay Islands of Honduras. Southern Caribbean cruises often sail out of San Juan, Puerto Rico, and ports of call might include any of the following: the US and British Virgin Islands, St Maarten/St Martin, St Kitts, Antigua, Guadeloupe, Dominica, St Lucia, Martinique, Grenada, Barbados and Trinidad & Tobago; smaller ships may also visit tiny Grenadine islands such as Bequia or Mayreau.

Greater Miami

Cruise port capital of the world, Miami is the gateway to the Caribbean, a cosmopolitan oceanfront city just a day trip away from the sunny Bahamas islands. It is a lively, modern metropolis, full of contrasts, cultural diversity and a whole host of tourist attractions and activities. Today, tourism is the city's number one industry, with some 11 million visitors a year. And around four million of these visitors will sail off into the sunset on board one of the 20 or so cruise ships which call the Port of Miami home.

Tourism in Miami began with the arrival of Henry Flagler's railroad in 1896. Florida folklore tells how Yankee pioneer Julia Tuttle intrigued Flagler by sending him fresh Miami orange blossom untouched by the Great Frost of 1894–5, that destroyed citrus groves as far south as Palm Beach. Flagler recognised the tourism potential of such a mild climate, extended his railroad south, and thus founded modern Miami.

During the early years of the 20th century, a handful of wealthy visitors established winter homes along the shore of Biscayne Bay. The grandest of these is James Deering's magnificent Vizcaya.

Then, inspired by the 1920s Florida land boom, George Merrick laid out America's first planned community, Coral Gables, which remains some of the most sought-after real estate in town. Meanwhile, a failed offshore avocado plantation was anchored to the mainland by causeways, and transformed into legendary Miami Beach.

Greater Miami covers a vast area of around 5,283sq km (2,040sq miles). At its heart, the skyscrapers of downtown Miami's business district provide a futuristic skyline but surprising pockets of early 20th-century charm also exist within the sprawling metropolis. These unexpected treats are often referred to as 'the neighbourhoods'.

The most famous is the pastel-painted Art Deco District on Miami Beach. Mainland Coconut Grove exudes a Bohemian air, while neighbouring Coral Gables boasts Mediterranean-style architecture, country clubs and tree-shaded avenues.

For local colour, look no further than the bustling Cuban district of Little Havana or discover the Caribbean-Creole influences in Little Haiti. However, a word of warning: after dark, the downtown business district is not recommended for wandering tourists, and nor is Little Haiti.

Miami (see pp36–7 for walk route)

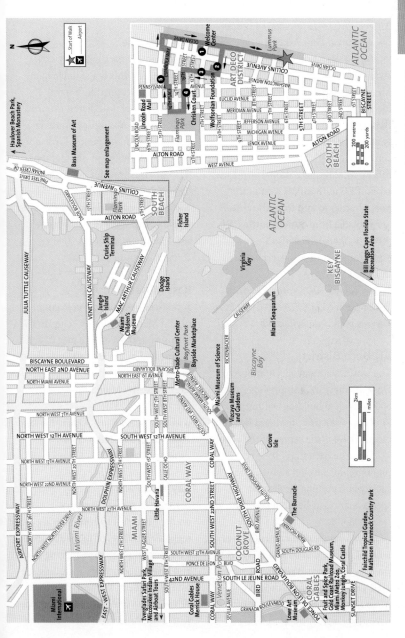

Greater Miami Convention & Visitors Bureau *701 Brickell Ave, Suite 2700, Miami, FL 33131. Tel: (305) 539 3000; www.miamiandbeaches.com*

Arrival

Miami's cruise ship port is centrally located in downtown Miami, near the Bayside Marketplace. Taxis are available at all the 12 terminals, and car rental companies offer shuttles to their off-site offices. Miami International airport is around 13km (8 miles) west of the port; shuttles to and from the airport are available from **SuperShuttle** (*Tel: 305/371 2000*), which also offers transfers to and from hotels in Dade County.

Port of Miami 1015 North American Way, Miami 33132. Tel: (305) 371 7678; www.co.miami-dade.fl.us/portofmiami

Art Deco District

The world's largest collection of Art Deco architecture, comprising some 800 individual buildings within a 2.5sq km (1sq mile) area on Miami Beach. Ocean Drive is the centre of the action – a favourite backdrop for photographic fashion shoots, café society and evening strolls past spectacular neon-lit hotel façades (*see pp36–7*).

*Maps, information and tours (with or without guides, and on foot or by bike) from the **Art Deco Welcome Center**, 1201 Ocean Drive, at 12th Street, Miami Beach. Tel: (305) 672 2014; www.mdpl.org. Open: Mon–Fri*

11am–6pm, Sat 10am–10pm, Sun 11am–10pm.

The Barnacle

Set in a lovely park with views over Biscayne Bay, this is a suitable name for a home designed by a naval architect. Ralph Middleton Munroe built this fine two-storey house in 1891. The inspired period furnishings include paintings and photographs.

3485 Main Highway, Coconut Grove. Tel: (305) 448 9445; www.floridastateparks.org/thebarnacle. Open: guided tours of the Barnacle Fri–Mon 10am, 11.30am, 1pm & 2.30pm. Admission charge.

Bass Museum of Art

A first-class permanent collection of Old Master paintings, sculpture, furniture and decorative arts is augmented by a wide-ranging calendar of special exhibitions.

2121 Park Ave, Miami Beach. Tel: (305) 673 7530; www.bassmuseum.org. Open: Tue–Sat 10am–5pm, Sun 11am–5pm. Admission charge.

Bayfront Park

A 13ha (32-acre) open space on the Biscayne bayfront offering magnificent views of the cruise ships, a concert amphitheatre, jogging paths and several memorials, including the John F Kennedy Memorial Torch of Friendship – symbolising Miami's ties with Latin America. There's also the

Miami Skylift, a passenger-carrying helium balloon that allows a bird's-eye view over the city.
101 Biscayne Blvd, Downtown (adjacent to Bayside Marketplace);
www.bayfrontparkmiami.com.
Skylift Sun–Thur 10am–7pm, Fri & Sat 10am–10pm. Admission charge.

Bayside Marketplace

This lively shopping, entertainment and dining complex overlooks the yachts moored in Miamarina. Browse around the 150 or so stores and the craft market, sample international cuisine, enjoy the antics of street performers, and tune in to the daily concerts.
401 North Biscayne Blvd.
Tel: (305) 577 3344;
www.baysidemarketplace.com.
Open: Mon–Thur 10am–10pm,
Fri & Sat 10am–11pm, Sun 11am–9pm;
extended hours at restaurants,
bars & cafés.

Bill Baggs Cape Florida State Recreation Area

This natural preserve at the tip of Key Biscayne has been planted with native South Florida trees and its 1.6km (1 mile) long sandy beach is one of the best spots on the bayfront. You'll find snack bars and barbecue areas plus bicycles, snorkelling gear and fishing tackle for hire.
1200 South Crandon Blvd, Key Biscayne.
Tel: (305) 361 5811;
www.floridastateparks.org. Open: daily 8am–sunset. Admission charge.

Coconut Grove

One of Miami's most attractive neighbourhoods, Coconut Grove is also one of the city's oldest. There were only two coconut palms in the 'grove' when Horace P Porter opened his Post Office here in 1873, while early visitors to the area stayed in rustic cabins along the shore. Today, the sidewalks may be brick and the streetlamps Victorian, but great shopping and good restaurants abound, and there's plenty of eye-catching architecture.

Coral Castle

A 20-year labour of love, this truly bizarre 1,100 ton carved coral rock edifice was built single-handedly by lovesick Latvian Edward Leedskalnin, and is said to be a memorial to the sweetheart who jilted him. It includes coral rock furniture, solar-heated bath tubs and a 9-ton gate.
28655 South Dixie Hwy, Homestead.

Tropical and subtropical plants surround George Merrick's former home

Tel: (305) 248 6345;
www.coralcastle.com. Open: Sun–Thur
8am–6pm, Fri & Sat 8am–9pm.
Admission charge.

Coral Gables Merrick House

The Merrick family home takes its
name from its Spanish-style roof tiles
made from local coral. Coral Gables'
founder, George Merrick, spent his
teens here, and many of the furnishings
and artefacts are genuine family pieces.
The pretty gardens have been planted
with a variety of native shrubs, scented
jasmine and fruit trees.
907 Coral Way, Coral Gables.
Tel: (305) 460 5361. Open: guided tours
Wed & Sun 1pm, 2pm & 3pm; gardens
daily until sunset. Admission charge.

Coral Gables Villages

A special feature of George Merrick's
'City Beautiful', these are small groups
of houses rather than villages in the real
sense, and some only cover a single
block. The tiny Chinese Village on
Maggiore Street features sweeping roofs
in green, yellow and blue, cut-out
oriental motifs and bamboo-design
window grilles. South on Hardee Road,
the French Country Village employs
towers, pointed slate 'witches-hat' roofs
and wooden shutters. Further south on
San Vicente Street, the pretty,
whitewashed Dutch Colonial Village
is particularly striking with its gables,
red-tiled roofs and twisted barley
sugar chimneys etched against a
deep blue sky.

The famous pink flamingoes at Jungle Island

Everglades Safari Park

Experience Florida's exotic 'river of
grass' by airboat. You can also explore
the jungle trails by foot, watch an
alligator and wildlife show and tour a
replica of a Cheekee Village.
26700 Tamiami Trail, Miami.
Tel: (305) 226 6923;
www.evsafaripark.com. Open: daily
9am–5pm. Admission charge.

Fairchild Tropical Garden

These botanical gardens are claimed to
be the largest in the continental USA,
including 34ha (83 acres) of tropical
plants, rolling lawns and clear lakes.
Narrated tram tours give an overview
of the grounds, and visitors are invited
to explore special rainforest, mangrove
and Everglades areas, as well as the rare
plant house.
10901 Old Cutler Rd, Coral Gables.
Tel: (305) 667 1651;
www.fairchildgarden.org. Open: daily
9.30am–4.30pm. Admission charge.

Fruit and Spice Park

There is a distinctly international flavour to this exotic 14.9ha (37-acre) site. More than 500 varieties of fruits, nuts, spices and herbs are cultivated here, from 150 different types of mango to 75 varieties of bananas.
24801 SW 187th Ave, Homestead.
Tel: (305) 247 5727;
www.fruitandspicepark.org.
Open: daily 9am–5pm.
Guided tours are available at 11am, 1.30pm and 3pm. Admission charge.

Gold Coast Railroad Museum

This collection of historic locomotives, rolling stock (including a presidential Pullman car used by presidents Roosevelt, Truman, Eisenhower, Reagan and George Bush Snr) and railroad memorabilia is just the ticket for train buffs. Train rides are a weekend highlight; kids will love the Link train.
12450 SW 152nd St, Kendall.
Tel: (305) 253 0063; www.gcrm.org.
Open: Mon–Fri 10am–4pm, Sat & Sun 11am–4pm. Admission charge.

Haulover Beach Park

A 1.5km (1-mile) stretch of natural dunes and seashore offering excellent facilities, including picnic areas, a children's playground, boat hire, family golf course, walking trails and tennis courts. Some areas of the beach are naturist.
10800 Collins Ave, North Miami Beach. Tel: (305) 947 3525;
www.miamidade.gov. Open: daily sunrise–sunset. Free admission.

Jungle Island

Jungle Island's brightly coloured cast of more than 1,000 exotic birds is complemented by orangutans, monkeys, snakes, spiders, crocodiles and tigers, many of which take part in regular shows throughout the day; you can also feed the famous pink flamingoes.
1111 Parrot Jungle Trail, Watson Island.
Tel: (305) 400 7000;
www.jungleisland.com. Open: daily 10am–6pm. Admission charge.

Lowe Art Museum

The exceptional Kress Collection of Renaissance and Baroque art is the highlight of this elegant small museum. It also features Spanish masterpieces, 19th- to 20th-century American works, Chinese porcelain, plus Asian, South American and Native American artefacts among its treasures, and stages regular temporary exhibitions.
1301 Stanford Drive, Coral Gables.
Tel: (305) 284 3535;
www.lowemuseum.org. Open: Tue, Wed, Fri & Sat 10am–5pm, Thur noon–7pm, Sun noon–5pm. Admission charge.

Matheson Hammock Country Park

A terrific bayside park with a beach, picnic tables, refreshments, walking

(*Cont. on p38*)

Architectural extravaganzas

Enthusiastic developers have long believed that anything is possible in Miami. Architects inspired by the vision of wide blue skies, exotic palm trees and balmy temperatures have been positively encouraged to let their imagination run riot. A happy result of this is that in addition to the famous Art Deco District (*see p36*), Miami is home to many other splendid and bizarre examples of 20th-century architecture.

Take, for instance, James Deering's Vizcaya (*see p39*). A short drive from the sheer glass and steel monuments to high finance of Brickell Avenue, this lavish 70-room Italianate villa, completed in 1918, is one of the earliest examples of the Miami construction boom.

Spanish-Mediterranean was the preferred style for Coral Gables, George Merrick's 'City Beautiful', founded in 1921. Among the special features here is the grand Puerto del Sol entrance, the enchanting Venetian Pool (*see p39*) and Merrick's pet project, The Villages. These seven enclaves of distinctive vernacular architecture range in style from Chinese and Italian to French and early Floridian. Unfortunately, an unnamed 1926 hurricane and the Depression of the 1930s prevented Merrick from completing many of his projects. The 90m (300ft) Spanish tower atop the imposing 1925 Biltmore Hotel is a local landmark.

Another themed community was Glenn Curtiss' Opa-Locka, a 1926 Moorish-style development in North Miami. Drawing inspiration from *1,001 Tales from the Arabian Nights*, Curtiss' architect was instructed to lay out streets in the shape of a crescent moon, and to adorn buildings with all manner of Moorish domes, minarets and painted tiles.

On a more classical note, elegant Hialeah Park is one of the most beautiful horse-racing courses in the world, with its ivy-covered French-style clubhouse, completed in 1932. The

The Italian-style Vizcaya

The towering Biltmore Hotel

eye-catching blue-and-white tiled façade of the Bacardi Imports Building (at 2100 Biscayne Boulevard) also dates from the 1930s (Barcardi moved out in 2009, but the City of Miami are taking steps to have it preserved as a historic building), while further south on the same street, the Freedom Tower strikes a surprise Old-World note on the Downtown skyline. It was built in 1925 for the Miami News as a copy of the Giralda Tower in Sevilla, Spain. Later, it was used to process Cuban refugees, hence the name.

The 1950s stamped their own style on Miami with such extravaganzas as the Fountainbleau Hotel (4441 Collins Ave). By this time, the small Art Deco hotels were considered passé and architects such as Morris Lapidus built hotels that affirmed the American spirit of the 1950s that 'bigger was better'. Even if you are not a guest, take time to wander through the lobby and spectacular pool, featured in the Bond film *Goldfinger*, just to feel the energy created by the army of bellhops, concierges and travellers.

The late decades of the 20th century saw skyscrapers swallow up much of the remaining land, but the waterfront has been preserved with plentiful park space and 'people places' such as Bayfront Park, with its gentle meandering curves. Who knows what new styles will become the hallmarks of the 21st century?

Walk: Art Deco District

In 1915, John Collins borrowed $50,000 and began to develop Miami Beach. As the mangrove wilderness was cleared, the first homes and hotels appeared, many built in the popular 1920s Mediterranean Revival-style. In the 1930s and 1940s, Miami Beach emerged as a showcase for the dashing new Art Deco architects. Rescued from decay in the 1970s, today's rejuvenated Art Deco District is one of the world's most fashionable places.

Allow 3 hours. See map on p29 for route.

Start on Ocean Drive at 6th St. Stroll up to the Art Deco Welcome Center.

1 Ocean Drive

Facing the ocean across Lummus Park and the beach, Ocean Drive unfurls in a magnificent sweep of Art Deco delights: streamlined façades, bold, vertical planes, racing stripes, 'eyebrow' windows and nautical and geometric motifs. The Park Central (No 630) employs all manner of these deco devices. Also note the namesake neon-lit tower atop the Waldorf (No 860) and ship's prow on the Breakwater (No 940).
Stop at the Welcome Center for information and maps, then head away from the beach on 10th St.

2 10th Street

A short walk down 10th Street leads to the Essex Hotel, with an etched glass flamingo on the porch door. Opposite, the Fairwind Hotel boasts extravagant neon. The huge Washington Storage Building (1001 Washington Ave), with its window grilles and Spanish Baroque-style carved reliefs, is now home to the Wolfsonian Foundation, which exhibits decorative and propaganda arts.
Tel: (305) 531 1001; www.wolfsonian.org. Open: Mon, Tue, Sat & Sun noon–6pm, Thur & Fri noon–9pm. Admission charge. Turn right on to Washington Ave.

3 Washington Avenue

Just north on Washington Avenue there is a clutch of modest 1930s hotels: the Park Washington, Taft and Kenmore (Nos 1020, 1044 and 1050), now all part of the Best Western chain. The 1927 Old City Hall (No 1130) is a nine-storey Mediterranean affair decorated with giant urns. Take a moment to visit the Depression Moderne-style Post Office (No 1300). Its rotunda has a mural and painted ceiling above the

semicircle of original brass mail boxes.
Walk west (left) on 13th St.

4 Apartment buildings

On 13th Street, pretty Chrisken Court
(No 541) features hefty wooden
balconies and decorative reliefs. The
Parkway Apartments, on the corner of
Meridian Avenue, enjoy a balconied
courtyard, colourful tiled steps and
niches filled with urns. The upper
section of Spanish-themed, gas-lit
Española Way has several restored
apartment houses such as the simple
Streamlined Allen (Nos 609–611) and
Mediterranean (Nos 531–525).
Walk north (right) on Meridian Ave, and
return east (right) on Española Way.

5 Española Way

From Drexel Avenue, William
Whitman's 1922 Spanish Village runs
for a block east on Española Way. The
tree-shaded sidewalks are lined with
cafés, boutiques, jewellers and retro
dealers selling second-hand clothes and
antiques beneath a cheerful array of
striped awnings and balconies. Take a
break here before returning to the top
end of Ocean Drive.
Cross Washington Ave, opposite the
Cameo Cinema (a model of 3-ton
Streamlined Vitralite). On the corner of
Collins Ave, turn left by the former
Hoffman's Cafeteria (No 1450), with its
distinctive cut-out corner façade. Take
the first right and rejoin Ocean Drive.

Walk: Art Deco District

Palm trees and candy-striped awnings shade shoppers on Española Way

trails and bike paths among the mangroves.
9610 Old Cutler Rd, Coral Gables. Tel: (305) 665 5475. Open: daily 8am–sunset. Admission charge for cars.

Metro-Dade Cultural Center

A landmark cultural centre which houses a trio of municipal showcases: the **Miami Art Museum** of Dade County, which focuses on Western art post-1945; the state-of-the-art **County Library**; and the admirable **Historical Museum of Southern Florida**. At the latter, life-sized dioramas depict 10,000 years of local history with the help of artefacts and hands-on displays.
101 West Flagler St, Downtown. Art Museum. Tel: (305) 375 1700; www.miamiartmuseum.org. Historical Museum. Tel: (305) 375 1492; www.hmsf.org. Open: Mon–Sat (except Art Museum, closed Mon) 10am–5pm (every third Thur until 9pm), Sun noon–5pm. Admission charge.

Miami Children's Museum

A thoughtful family alternative to the theme parks, with two floors of interactive exhibits, from a climbable two-storey sandcastle to a TV studio and a climbing wall.
980 MacArthur Causeway, Watson Island. Tel: (305) 375 5437; www.miamichildrensmuseum.org. Open: daily 10am–6pm. Admission charge.

Miami Metro Zoo

This is one of the largest 'cageless' zoos in the USA. Natural habitats have been created to simulate the African veld and jungle, and there's also the brand new Amazon and Beyond exhibit, divided into Cloud, Amazon and Atlantic forest sections. A 3km (2 mile) monorail circuit ensures a bird's-eye view of the residents.
12400 SW 152nd St, South Miami. Tel: (305) 251 0400; www.miamimetrozoo.com. Open: daily 9.30am–5.30pm. Admission charge.

Miami Museum of Science and Space Transit Planetarium

A gripping voyage of exploration through the mysteries of science and space enlivened by more than 140 hands-on displays, multimedia shows, robotic dinosaurs, virtual reality basketball and a planetarium.
3280 South Miami Ave, Coconut Grove. Tel: (305) 646 4200; www.miamisci.org. Open: daily 10am–6pm. Admission charge.

Miami Seaquarium

A fun outing for all the family, the Seaquarium offers an educational look at the marine world with exciting shows. Check out the manatees, swim with dolphins, dip into the touch tanks, watch the shark-feeding and take your seats for Lolita the killer whale, TV star Flipper the dolphin, and the comical Salty the Sea Lion show.
4400 Rickenbacker Causeway.

Tel: (305) 361 5705;
www.miamiseaquarium.com.
Open: daily 9.30am–6pm.
Admission charge.

Monkey Jungle

In 1933, animal behaviourist Joe Dumond released six macaque monkeys in a 4ha (10-acre) hardwood hammock (small wood) intending to study their habits. However, running short of funds he caged in walkways for visitors and the free-ranging macaque colony developed into a popular attraction, which includes an 'Amazonian Rainforest' section, with hordes of rare plants. Now, around 500 primates (mostly running free) represent 30 species of monkeys, and you can watch them dive into a pool to get fruit at feeding times.
14805 SW 216th St, Homestead.
Tel: (305) 235 1611;
www.monkeyjungle.com.
Open: daily 9.30am–5pm.
Admission charge.

Spanish Monastery

Strange but true: Miami is the unlikely site of the oldest building in the USA. Newspaper magnate William Randolph Hearst bought the 12th-century cloisters of St Bernard's Monastery and shipped them from Segovia, Spain, in 1929. Re-erected in 1954, they now serve as an Episcopal church.
16711 West Dixie Hwy, North Miami Beach. Tel: (305) 945 1461;
www.spanishmonastery.com.
Open: guided tours Mon–Sat

9am–4.30pm, Sun noon–4.30pm.
Admission charge.

Venetian Pool

This Venetian-inspired lagoon, newly renovated and complete with little humpbacked bridges, grottoes and waterfalls, is one of the most unusual and delightful swimming pools imaginable. In its heyday, the Miami Opera, Tarzan star Johnny Weissmuller and bathing belle Esther Williams all performed here. Now visitors can bask on the sandy beach, bathe in the crystal-clear water fed by a natural spring, and find refreshments in the courtyard café.
2701 De Soto Blvd, Coral Gables.
Tel: (305) 460 5306;
www.coralgablesvenetianpool.com.
Open: Tue–Fri 11am–5.30pm
(till 7.30pm in July and early Aug),
Sat & Sun 10am–4.30pm.
Admission charge.

Vizcaya Museum and Gardens

Built between 1916 and 1918 as a winter home for industrialist James Deering, this palatial Italian Renaissance-style villa is one of Miami's finest attractions. It is set back from Biscayne Bay in 4ha (10 acres) of formal landscaped gardens, and acts as a showcase for Deering's treasure trove of 15th- to 19th-century antiques.
3251 South Miami Ave, Coconut Grove.
Tel: (305) 250 9133;
www.vizcayamuseum.org. Open: daily 9.30am–4.30pm. Admission charge.

Fort Lauderdale

*An hour's journey (and 37km/23 miles) north of Miami,
Fort Lauderdale is one of Florida's leading beach resorts,
and its five-star cruise facility, Port Everglades, serves
between 3 and 4 million cruise passengers each year
(though, confusingly, it's nowhere near the Everglades).
Fort Lauderdale is all glitter, from the tips of its Downtown
skyscrapers to the maze of sparkly waterways that have
earned it the nickname the 'Venice of America'. It is also
one of the fastest growing cities in the state.*

The first settlers

The city is named after Major William Lauderdale, who established the first of three small forts here in the 1830s. In 1893, pioneer settler Frank Stranahan established an overnight camp for the Bay Biscayne Stagecoach Line, and traded provisions for alligator hides, pelts and egret plumes brought to him by the local Seminole Indians. With the arrival of the railroad in 1896, a small settlement grew around the trading post and attracted the attention of Florida State Governor Napoleon Bonaparte Broward, who unveiled a grand plan to drain the Everglades.

Dredging operations began along the New River in 1906. Then, during the 1920s land boom, a Venetian land-building technique, known as 'finger-islanding', was used to transform the mangrove swamps between the river and the Intracoastal Waterway into a network of channels and building plots. Today, the city's 200km (300 miles) of navigable inland waterways are one of its top attractions, plied by sightseeing boats, private yachts and a handy water-taxi service.

Golden opportunities

From the 1950s through to the 1970s, Fort Lauderdale was infamous for its raucous spring break student parties. However, following a clampdown by the authorities, the students have moved on and the city has emerged as a popular year-round family tourist destination.

Together with its neighbouring beachside communities, Greater Fort Lauderdale offers 37km (23 miles) of golden beaches, historic homes, modern museums, fine shopping and a range of family attractions. Top-class facilities, such as the magnificent Broward Center for the Performing Arts, complement the city's dynamic cultural programme.

For outdoor types, there are sporting opportunities galore, from golf, diving, sailing and sport fishing to tennis.

Spectators can enjoy such fast and furious sports as jai-alai (a version of the Basque pelota, involving a small ball being hurled at speeds of up to 280kph/175mph with the aid of curved wicker slings attached to players' hands) at Dania, horse-racing at Gulfstream Park and weekly rodeos in Davie. *Information from Greater Fort Lauderdale Convention and Visitors Bureau. 100 East Broward Boulevard, Suite 200, Fort Lauderdale, Florida 33301. Tel: (954) 765 4466; www.sunny.org*

Arrival

Port Everglades is one of the world's largest, busiest ports, serving container ships as well as cruisers, and its 11 passenger terminals are spread over a large area to the south of downtown Fort Lauderdale. Taxis are available at the terminals for the run to Fort Lauderdale, and buses stop at the Northern section of the port. Most local car rental companies provide shuttles from the port to their off-site locations. The Fort Lauderdale–Hollywood International Airport is 3km (2 miles) south of the port. Airport shuttles run to and from Port Everglades; call (974) 791 6575 to book. *Port Everglades. 1850 Eller Drive. Tel: (954) 523 3404; www.porteverglades.net.*

Bonnet House

This lovely plantation-style house is set in a leafy 15ha (35-acre) estate, just a stone's throw from the Downtown skyscrapers. Artists Frederick Clay Bartlett and his wife, Evelyn, designed the eclectic and unusual interior with a rich collection of decorative and fine arts. Namesake bonnet lilies grow around a miniature lake in the grounds. *900 N Birch Rd. Tel: (954) 563 5393; www.bonnethouse.org. Open: guided tours only, Tue–Sat 10am–4pm, Sun noon–4pm. Closed: Mon. Admission charge.*

Butterfly World

This popular attraction provides a dazzling insight into the insect world. Around 150 species of butterflies inhabit huge walk-through aviaries, planted with tropical foliage. There's also an insectarium, a museum and the USA's largest free-flight hummingbird aviary. *Tradewinds Park South, 3600 W Sample Rd, Coconut Creek. Tel: (954) 977 4400; www.butterflyworld.com. Open: Mon–Sat 9am–5pm, Sun 11am–5pm. Admission charge.*

Everglades Holiday Park Airboat Tours

Skim across the shallow marshes on an airboat for a real Everglades experience, which includes a visit to a replica Seminole Indian village and views of Southern Florida's unique flora and fauna. *21940 Griffin Rd. Tel: (954) 434 8111; www.evergladesholidaypark.com. Open: daily tours every 30 minutes from 9am–5pm. Admission charge.*

Flamingo Gardens

One of the area's earliest citrus groves has been transformed into a splendid garden bursting with exotic blooms and towering trees inhabited by a collection of animals and birds including monkeys, crocodiles, alligators and, of course, flamingoes.

A tram ride explores the 24ha (60-acre) site, which also boasts a bird of prey centre, museum and shop. *3750 Flamingo Rd, Davie. Tel: (954) 473 2955; www.flamingogardens.org. Open: daily 9.30–5.30pm. Closed: Mon 1 June– 30 Sept. Admission charge.*

The courtyard of Bonnet House

Hugh Taylor Birch State Recreation Area

A 73ha (180-acre) green breathing space, locked between the beachfront and Intracoastal Waterway. Walk or cycle around the 3km (2-mile) circuit, investigate the short hardwood hammock trail, or rent a canoe and look out for raccoons, marsh rabbits and wading birds. A short film show at the visitor centre gives a potted history and introduction to the park, and there's access to the beach via a pedestrian tunnel under the waterway.

3109 E Sunrise Blvd. Tel: (954) 564 4521; www.floridastateparks.org/ hughtaylorbirch. Open: daily 8am–dusk. Admission charge.

International Swimming Hall of Fame and Aquatic Complex

The Hall of Fame features a terrific array of swimming memorabilia in its museum wing. There are displays on all-time greats such as Johnny 'Tarzan' Weissmuller and Mark Spitz, plus Olympic gold medals, swimwear through the ages and much more. The Aquatic Complex, with its two Olympic pools and diving facilities, is patronised by Olympic hopefuls and it is also open to the lap-swimming public.

501 Seabreeze Blvd. Tel: (954) 828 4580; www.ishof.org; http://ci.ftlaud.fl.us/flac. Open: Hall of Fame daily 9am–5pm; Aquatic Complex Mon–Fri 8am–4pm & 6–7.30pm, Sat & Sun 8am–2pm. Admission charge.

Jungle Queen

This old-style riverboat offers daily sightseeing cruises around the waterways of the 'Venice of America'. It glides past exclusive waterfront homes and stops off at a purpose-built Indian Village for a spot of alligator wrestling and souvenir shopping. At night, sail up the New River for a 'Bar-B-Que Ribs, Chicken & Shrimp Dinner Cruise' on a private island, an all-you-can-eat spread with entertainment in the form of a vaudeville show and an old-fashioned singalong.

TROLLEY TOURS AND WATER TAXIS

There are two great ways to get around Fort Lauderdale and see the sights: **South Florida Trolley Tours** offers daily narrated historical tours in old San Francisco-style trams with pick-ups from all major hotels (*tel: (954) 492 3100 for information*).

Fort Lauderdale's **water taxis** run between the docks at Oakland Park Boulevard and Southeast 17th Street along the Intracoastal Waterway, and west along the New River into downtown Fort Lauderdale as far as Las Olas Riverfront, stopping at key hotel, shopping and dining locations along the way. The service operates daily from 10am until midnight, and the set fare allows unlimited rides all day. The South Beach Express connects Fort Lauderdale with Miami, stopping at the Bayside Marketplace and the Miami Beach Marina, convenient for Ocean Drive.

You can pick up a taxi from the dock in the port, or call the operator (*tel: (954) 467 6677; www.watertaxi.com*) and make a booking.

Las Olas Boulevard is a shopper's paradise

*Bahia Mar Yacht Center (off A1A), 801
Seabreeze Boulevard, Fort Lauderdale
Beach. Tel: (954) 462 5596;
www.junglequeen.com*

Las Olas Boulevard

Fort Lauderdale's prettiest shopping
street is a must on any holiday-maker's
itinerary. Landscaped with flowers and

trees, the one mile (1.6km) long boulevard is studded with a host of chic designer boutiques, art and antiques galleries and attractive restaurants.

Museum of Art

This state-of-the-art showcase is renowned for its fine collections of 19th- and 20th-century American and European paintings and sculpture. In addition, there are collections of ethnic art, and the gallery stages some interesting temporary exhibitions, as well as hosting an Artist in Residence programme. Drop in at the excellent museum store, too.

1 E Las Olas Blvd, Downtown.
Tel: (954) 525 5500; www.moafl.org.
Open: Fri–Wed 11am–7pm, Thur
11am–9pm, June–Nov closed Mon.
Admission charge.

Museum of Discovery and Science

A high-tech 'hands-on' museum packed with marvellous gadgets, games and educational exhibits which make learning lots of fun. There are seven display areas, ranging from the high-tech Runways to Rockets to the grassroots Florida EcoScapes with its walk-through guide to local habitats. Programme a robot, take a space ride on the Meteor Storm, or goggle in amazement at the five-storey-high IMAX cinema screen.

401 SW 2nd St. Tel: (954) 467 6637;
www.mods.org. Open: Mon–Sat
10am–5pm, Sun noon–6pm.
Admission charge.

Riverwalk

The landscaped Riverwalk was part of the city's massive multi-million dollar urban redesign programme for the 1990s and provides access to Fort Lauderdale's prime river frontage. Stroll westwards along the New River from Stranahan House up to the historic Himmarshee Village area and Broward Center for the Performing Arts, stopping off to admire the views from an outdoor café, picnic table or park bench.

Stranahan House

The oldest house in Broward County, this homely pioneer property was built on the banks of the New River in 1900 and served as a post office, town hall and meeting house. Trader Frank Stranahan and his schoolteacher wife, Ivy Cromatie, lived here, and once entertained East Coast railway baron Henry Flagler in the pine panelled living room. The interior has been restored in the style of 1913–15, with antique Victorian furniture and period pieces, together with photographs of Fort Lauderdale's early days. There's also a 'River Ghost Tour' boat trip on Sunday evenings. The tour includes entry to the house and is very popular; book ahead.

335 E Las Olas Blvd (at SE 6th Ave).
Tel: (954) 524 4736;
www.stranahanhouse.org.
Open: guided tours only
Wed–Sun 1pm, 2pm & 3pm.
Admission charge.

The Everglades

The Native Americans called it *pa-hay-okee* or 'grassy waters', a very apt name for this vast, waterlogged region that stretches from Lake Okeechobee in the north down to Florida Bay and the Gulf of Mexico. The endless vista of rippling, razor-sharp sawgrass was once a hideout for Seminole Indians who travelled the maze of secret waterways. Today, it is the last refuge of the rare Florida panther and a haven for other endangered species such as the Everglades mink, American crocodile and alligator, roseate spoonbill, bald eagle and osprey.

The best time to visit the Everglades is during the dry winter season. Wildlife spotting is easier as the animals and birds gather around the deepwater sloughs (waterholes) to feed, and there are fewer mosquitoes to trouble you (but don't leave off the heavy-duty repellent even in winter). More than 2,000 plant species flourish in the subtropical conditions, and 45 of these are unique to the region. Rising above the marshy grasslands, shady hammocks (small woods) of willow, pine and tropical hardwoods such as mahogany and live oak cling to limestone outcrops, providing shelter for wildlife and a host for airplants, such as orchids and bromeliads. A less welcome guest is the parasitic strangler fig, dropping its tangled aerial roots to the ground and gradually depriving the host tree of water and light until it dies. Stands of elegant cypress trees are mirrored in the tannin-rich waters of quiet swamps.

The Everglades are home to the American crocodile

The Everglades is itself endangered. Starting in the 1930s, a giant flood control system began diverting water to canals running to the gulf and the ocean. The Everglades is now networked by 1,700 miles (2,735km) of canals and levees, and more than half of the total original area has been lost to development. The unfortunate side effect of building and flood control has been a devastation of the wilderness. Birds have diminished, the black bear has been eliminated and the Florida panther is almost extinct.

Serious steps are being taken to help both the cities and the Everglades live in harmony with each other. In 1947 Everglades National Park was created to preserve the slow-moving 'river of grass'.

More than a score of government agencies and private conservation groups, in concert with industry, are now working feverishly to secure the future of the Everglades. The next decade will determine its success or failure. For more information and updates, visit the Everglades Restoration Plan website, *www.evergladesplan.org*

A visit to the Everglades is an unmissable experience. Allow a full day to visit the Everglades National Park from Miami or Fort Lauderdale. The main entrance and **Park Information Center** (*Tel: (305) 242 7700. Open: daily*

Everglades National Park is one of the world's most outstanding natural habitats

8am–5pm) lie 16km (10 miles) southwest of Florida City. The information centre shows an introductory film and provides brochures, maps, details of boat tours, canoe rentals and guided walks which depart from the Royal Palm Interpretive Center. The northern entrance to the park is at Shark Valley, 56km (35 miles) west of Downtown Miami via the Tamiami Trail (US41). The Information Center (*Tel: (305) 221 8776; www.nps.gov/ever. Open: daily 9am–5pm*) can advise on trails, bicycle rental and tram tours.

Key West

The southernmost city in the USA, Key West is a popular stop with several cruise lines operating in the Caribbean. Measuring just 6.5km by 3km (4 miles by 2 miles), Key West remains at heart a village (albeit a rather exotic one). It is a quirky mix of old and new. Once the haunt of pirates and wreckers (more politely known as ship's salvagers), it is now a popular gay enclave and welcomes the annual winter invasion of tourists with amused tolerance.

While walking is the best way to savour the charms and relaxed atmosphere of Old Key West (the central hub of town), you can also be ferried around the main island sights aboard the Old Town Trolley, or take a 90-minute narrated tour on the Conch Train. Should you be ashore at dusk, the sunset celebrations on Mallory Dock, performed by a host of wacky street entertainers and musicians, are a near-legendary institution.

Arrival

There are three cruise ship docks on Key West, all on the western (Gulf) side of the island. Mallory Square and the Hilton hotel's Pier B are both in the heart of the Old Town and within walking distance of shops, restaurants and bars of Duval and Whitehead streets. The Outer Mall pier is a little further from the action, and there's a shuttle service from the dock to Mallory Square. Key West's tiny dimensions mean you're unlikely to want to use taxis, instead exploring by foot; however, they are available at the docks. The **Conch Tour Train** departs from Front Street and ends at Mallory Square, while the Old Town Trolley meets boats at the dock.

Conch Tour Train. Tel: (305) 294 5161; www.conchtourtrain.com

Old Town Trolley. Tel: 1800 868 7482, www.trolleytours.com

Fort Zachary Taylor State Historic Site

Founded in 1845, Fort Zachary Taylor was a rare Union outpost in the south during the Civil War. Rescued from obscurity, it now houses a small museum and a large collection of Civil War cannons. On the shore, there is a public beach with picnic tables in the shade and a restaurant.

Southard St, in the Truman Annex. Tel: (305) 292 6713. www.floridastateparks.org/forttaylor/. Open: daily 8am–dusk. Admission charge.

Eco-Discovery Centre

A great opportunity to get some insight into the unique ecosystem of the Florida Keys, with displays on everything from mangroves to coral reefs, a 2,500-gallon reef tank with living corals and tropical fish, and a mock-up of Aquarius, the world's only underwater ocean laboratory.
35 East Quay Road. Tel: (305) 809 4750, floridakeys.noaa.gov. Open: Tue–Sat 9am–4pm.

Hemingway House

Ernest Hemingway moved into this mid-19th-century house in 1931 with his second wife, Pauline, and they furnished it with a mixture of Spanish, Cuban and African mementoes from their travels. The author wrote most of his finest work here, and his eight-toed cats' descendants still have the run of the place. The guided tours impart a wealth of anecdotal information.
907 Whitehead St. Tel: (305) 294 1136; www.hemingwayhome.com.
Open: daily 9am–5pm.
Admission charge.

Key West Aquarium

A local attraction since 1934, offering aquariums, touch tanks, turtle pens and shark-feeding opportunities (*11am, 1pm, 3pm & 4.30pm*) for fearless visitors.
1 Whitehead St. Tel: 1-800 868 7482; www.keywestaquarium.com.
Open: daily 10am–6pm.
Admission charge.

Key West Lighthouse Museum

This 1848 lighthouse affords splendid views over Key West and the coast from its viewing balcony, reached by way of 88 steps. There is an interesting small museum in the former Keeper's Quarters.
938 Whitehead St.
Tel: (305) 294 0012;
www.kwahs.com.
Open: daily 9.30am–4.30pm.
Admission charge.

Mel Fisher Maritime Heritage Museum

Gold bullion, jewellery, silver tableware, and other treasures salvaged from Spanish wrecks by Key West's most famous treasure hunter, Mel Fisher, are on display at this fascinating maritime museum.
200 Greene St. Tel: (305) 294 2633;
www.melfisher.org. Open: Mon–Fri 8.30am–5pm, Sat & Sun 9.30am–5pm.
Admission charge.

Wrecker's Museum

Key West's oldest house, this 1829 sea captain's home evokes a distinctly nautical air. It contains period furnishings and all manner of artefacts, model ships, pictures and documents relating to the 19th-century wrecking (that is, salvage) industry.
322 Duval St.
Tel: (305) 294 9501;
www.oirf.org.
Open: Thur–Sat 10am–2pm.
Admission charge.

Antigua

The largest of the Leeward Islands, Antigua (pronounced An-tee-ga) combines some of the Caribbean's finest white sand beaches with several interesting historical sites. The island was sighted by Christopher Columbus on his second voyage to the New World in 1493, and named after Santa María de la Antigua, a miraculous statue of the Virgin in Seville Cathedral.

Its earliest inhabitants were Stone Age Ciboney people who migrated from South America around 4,000 years ago. The Ciboneys, and their successors, the Arawaks, left their mark on several Amerindian sites, especially around Indian Creek. An English colony from St Kitts established the first permanent European settlement here in 1632 and, except for two brief periods of occupation by the French and Spanish, Antigua remained linked to Britain until full independence in 1981.

Antigua's scalloped, irregular coastline is one of its chief delights. They say there are 365 beaches – one for every day of the year. Fine, natural harbours such as St John's, Falmouth and English Harbour have welcomed sailors for generations, and sailing is still big on the island.

The Caribbean's winter sailing calendar culminates in April/May with Antigua Sailing Week, a major international regatta and week-long celebration.

Antigua Department of Tourism
Govt. Complex, Queen Elizabeth Hwy. PO Box 363, St John's. Tel: (268) 462 0480; www.antigua-barbuda.org. There is also a tourist information booth on the dock at Heritage Quay, St John's. and another in the mall itself, on the first floor at 25 Heritage Quay.

Arrival

The cruise ship dock is adjacent to Heritage Quay shopping centre on St John's, from where you can easily explore the town on foot. If there are several ships in port, you may dock at the Deep Water Harbour on the southwest side of the St John's harbour, from where it's a 1.5km (1-mile) drive to St John's proper. Taxis offering island excursions park on the road just outside Heritage Quay, and drivers can act as guides. All taxis are unmetered, so agree on a price before you set out. There are limited bus services to most points in the island departing from the Western Bus Station, adjacent to the

Antigua

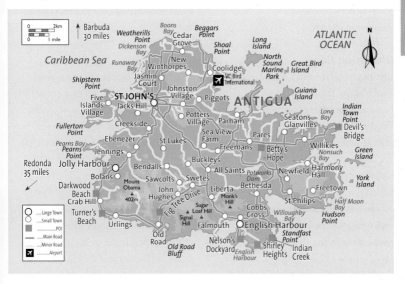

market, and the Eastern Bus Station, near to the cathedral, but as there are no timetables, getting back to the ship on time isn't guaranteed.

St John's

The entrance to St John's Harbour is guarded by Fort Barrington and Fort James, two of the numerous 18th-century defensive structures built by the British.

Behind the forts, the attractive West Indian town climbs gently back from the wharf in an attractive jumble of clapboard houses, fretwork balconies and roadside stalls to **St John's Cathedral**.

The impressive church building is flanked by its twin towers topped with silver cupolas. Erected in the mid-19th century on the site of two previous churches, the dignified wooden interior is worth a visit for its barrel ceilings supported by octagonal pillars, the decorative upper gallery, and grand memorials bedecked with coats of arms and purple prose.

Church Lane. Free admission.

Museum of Antigua and Barbuda

Housed in the Old Court House, built in 1750, this small museum traces the history of Antigua and its tiny sister island Barbuda. Relics of the ancient Ciboney and Arawak Indians include grinding stones, axe heads and conch shell chisels. There are sections on the plantation era, local flora and birdlife, but pride of place goes to the cricket bat of former West Indies and Antigua cricket captain Viv Richards.

Corner of Market & Long Sts. Tel: (268) 462 1469; www.antiguamuseums.org.

Open: Mon–Thur 8.30am–3pm, Fri 9am–4pm, Sat 9am–2pm. Admission charge.

Dickenson Bay

Just north of St John's, Fort James Beach is the closest beach to the capital, but many short-stay visitors prefer to head a little further north to the resort area at Runaway Bay and the adjacent Dickenson Bay. Both provide silky sand and clear waters, while the latter has watersports including windsurf and Hobie Cat (catamaran) hire, plus a welcome choice of beachside bars and restaurants in the shade.

Darkwood Beach and Crab Hill

A Caribbean idyll – a crescent of soft, pale sand bordering clear, turquoise waters and fringed by palms – Dark Wood Beach is almost deserted during the week, but busy at the weekend. There are good beach side restaurants here and at the adjacent Turner's Beach, further south and capped by Johnson's Point. Another quiet and beautiful sand strip on Crab Hill Bay, it offers some great snorkelling over the reefs around the point.

Fig Tree Drive

Past Turner's beach, the coast road swings inland onto this rare corner of natural vegetation. The most scenic road on the island, Fig Tree Drive escaped the 17th- and 18th-century sugar-cane boom and is lined with palms and banana plants. Halfway along, the Rainforest Canopy Tour offers a fun way to get up close to the forest, with a system of nine zipwires strung between the trees.

*Inland of Swetes and Old Road, south coast. Canopy Tour: Tel: (268) 562 6363; www.antiguarainforest.com.
Open: 8am–6pm daily.
Admission charge.*

English Harbour and Falmouth

One of the safest natural anchorages in the world, English Harbour was the British Admiralty's Caribbean base throughout the 18th and 19th centuries.

Looking out over English Harbour from Shirley Heights, Antigua

Pillars from a former sail loft in the garden of the Admiral's Inn, Nelson's Dockyard

Falmouth, nearby, was once the capital of Antigua, and the two bays, divided by a narrow isthmus fortified by the British, are now busy yachting anchorages during the winter season.

Horatio Nelson was posted to English Harbour in 1784. The young captain of HMS *Boreas*, a 28-gun frigate, was not amused. He considered Antigua a 'barbarous place', and fell out with the locals for enforcing the Navigation Act (banning trade with US vessels) too vigorously. Angry businessmen sued him for loss of earnings, and the future naval hero was forced to spend eight weeks on board his ship to avoid imprisonment. John Herbert of the Montpelier Plantation, Nevis (*see p119*), put up Nelson's £10,000 bail, and when he went ashore to dine with his benefactor, Nelson met his wife-to-be, Fanny Nesbit. At the wedding, Fanny was given away by Nelson's friend Prince William Henry, later King William IV, who lived at

Clarence House overlooking the harbour. Despite Nelson's aversion to the place, his name lingers on at Nelson's Dockyard.
South coast, via All Saints.

Nelson's Dockyard

This splendidly restored Georgian dockyard, which served as the British naval base in the Eastern Caribbean during the colonial era, was abandoned by the British Navy in 1889. In the 1960s it was returned to its present spick-and-span state of grey-shuttered stone and wooden buildings, and is now a lively and atmospheric marina as well as a historic attraction.

Just inside the gates, a former pitch, tar and turpentine store has been transformed into the Admiral's Inn, a small hotel. The 16 massive pillars in its gardens once supported a sail loft: boats would berth in the narrow dock below while their sails were whipped up into an overhead loft for repair. At the

Dockyard Museum in the Admiral's House, displays chart the history of the area and of Nelson's stint here, while the adjacent Copper and Lumber Store, with its flower-wreathed internal courtyard, has been converted into another hotel. An attractive two-storey brick building built over huge cisterns used to store water, the former 1821 Officers' Quarters now houses a restaurant on its upper floor. Scattered around the site are various remains of the dockyard days, from the massive Camelford Anchor to three huge capstans, used to haul down ships' masts during careening, while various outbuildings hold craft shops and a bar.

Tel: (268) 460 1379; www.antiguamuseums.com. Open: daily 8am–6pm. Admission charge, covers Dow's Hill and the Blockhouse.

Shirley Heights

Named after General Sir Thomas Shirley, Governor of the Leeward Islands between 1781 and 1791, the fortified hills above English Harbour afford a magnificent view over the sheltered bays and across to the island of Guadeloupe. Remains of the 18th-century signal station, which could give advance warning of a French attack, and the once sizeable military complex are scattered over a large area. About halfway up the hill, the Dow's Hill Interpretation Centre has a 15-minute multimedia presentation depicting scenes from Antiguan history, which traces the island's settlement by South American Indians, through the European Age of Discovery and Plantation era to the present day. There are fantastic views from the lookout point outside, perched on the ruins of the Belvedere, the 18th-century governor's residence.

Just east of, and overlooking, English Harbour. Tel: (268) 460 2777. Open: daily 9am–5pm. Admission charge, covers Dow's Hill, Cape Shirley and the Blockhouse.

Naval Officers' House in Nelson's Dockyard, English Harbour

Cape Shirley and the Blockhouse

At the very top of Shirley Heights, Cape Shirley is a barren and windblown spot that affords panoramic views over the southeast coast to Mamora and Willoughby Bays; the house ranged over the cliffs at Standfast Point, the closest promontory, belongs to rock star Eric Clapton. On a clear day, Montserrat and Guadeloupe are also visible. The collection of buildings here are known collectively as the Blockhouse; most are ruined, though a couple – such as the boxy Guardhouse – have been painstakingly restored.

The north and east

If you want to explore far from the madding crowd, there are several pleasant spots dotted over the eastern side of the island.

Betty's Hope

Betty's Hope was one of Antigua's chief 17th-century sugar plantations. Among the ruins, a stone windmill and its machinery have been restored and there is a small museum in the visitors' centre.
Off the central island road to Indian Creek. Tel: (268) 462 1469; www.antiguamuseums.org. Open: Tues–Sat 9am–4pm. Admission charge.

Harmony Hall

This fine, old stone house, built around a sugar mill, is a perfect spot for shopping and lunch, and you can even take a dip in the swimming pool. This

Palm-fringed Dark Wood Beach on Antigua's southwest coast

is principally an art gallery selling the work of local artists and high-quality Caribbean crafts. There is a breezy bar and lookout point in the old mill overlooking Nonsuch Bay.
East coast. Tel: (268) 460 4120; www.harmonyhallantigua.com. Open: early Nov to mid May daily 9am–6pm. Free admission.

Indian Creek National Park

It's a scenic drive across the east coast and Indian Creek National Park, where the Atlantic surf has carved blowholes and an impressive arch, known as Devil's Bridge, out of the limestone cliffs. This is a spectacular place on a blustery day, with great views of the islands offshore, and a lovely beach nearby at Long Bay.
Northeast coast.

Parham

In the middle of the north coast, Parham, a small fishing village with an unusual octagonal church, is one of the oldest settlements on Antigua.
Central north coast.

The Bahamas

On 12 October 1492, Christopher Columbus discovered the New World. He is said to have made landfall on the Bahamanian island of Guanahani, which he named San Salvador. North and east of the Caribbean proper, the 700 islands and 2,000-plus cays which comprise the Bahama Islands lie scattered across 260,000sq km (100,000sq miles) of Atlantic Ocean. Only around 30 of the islands are inhabited.

Originally, the archipelago was named the Lucayans, after the local Arawak people; the word Bahamas comes from the Spanish *baja-mar*, meaning 'shallow sea'. These flat, barren, coral rock islands were ignored by the Spanish and claimed by the British, who under the leadership of William Sayle founded a Puritan settlement on Eleuthera in 1648. This initial settlement was a failure, but Sayle discovered a fine natural harbour on the adjacent New Providence island where a fort and city (later called Nassau) sprang up. Within a few years, however, it had developed into a buccaneer base frequented by the likes of Blackbeard and Jack Rackham. Finally, pirate-turned-governor Woodes Rogers was enlisted by the British government to bring the colony under control in the 1720s, curtailing the privateers' raids. During the American War of Independence, the islands proved a useful source of arms for the rebels, and afterwards they welcomed fleeing loyalists who arrived with their slaves to set up plantations. Further fortunes were made from gun-running during the Civil War, and from bootleg booze during Prohibition. Since World War II, the Bahamas have experienced a tourist boom concentrated on the islands of Grand Bahama and New Providence. The billion-dollar industry employs around two-thirds of the workforce, who do not pay taxes, thanks to the revenue generated by offshore finance and ships' registry fees.

GRAND BAHAMA

From a handful of sleepy fishing villages to a major holiday destination within the space of 30 years, Grand Bahama, the fourth largest Bahamanian island, is one of the region's top tourist spots. More than a million visitors come every year, lured by its miles of white sand beaches and duty-free shopping.

Grand Bahama Tourist Office
PO Box F40251, International Bazaar, Freeport. Tel: (242) 302 2000.

Bahamas Ministry of Tourism *PO Box N3701, Nassau. Tel: (242) 322 7500.*
Rawson Square Tourist Information Booth Nassau *Tel: (242) 326 9781. Also see: www.bahamas.com*

Arrival

Ships dock at Lucayan Harbour, ten minutes' drive west of Freeport and within walking distance of the shops and restaurants of Port Lucaya Marketplace and Lucaya Beach. Taxis wait at the port whenever a ship is in dock to take you to Freeport, Lucaya or further afield; fares are fixed.

Freeport and Lucaya

American entrepreneur Wallace Groves was the man behind Grand Bahama's transformation. The sprawling, modern city of Freeport, together with its beach resort annexe, Lucaya, is very much based on the American model. Its broad boulevards, shopping malls and high-rise hotels are anything but Caribbean.

Garden of the Groves and Grand Bahama Museum

On the eastern outskirts of Freeport, this lush 5ha (12-acre) garden was laid out in honour of Mr and Mrs Wallace Groves. It is landscaped with over 510,000 varieties of flowers, shrubs and trees, pools fed by miniature waterfalls, meandering paths and plenty of quiet corners, including a pretty chapel at the top of the hill, a popular place for weddings; and a newly built labyrinth, intended as a place of meditation and relaxation.

Midshipman Rd. Tel: (242) 373 5668.
Open: daily 9am–5pm, open until 10pm on Fridays. Admission charge.

International Bazaar

A 4ha (10-acre) shoppers' paradise, the architecture here could best be described as 'international bizarre'. It was built in 1967 as the brainchild of a Hollywood special effects set designer, and houses an international cast of boutiques and stores which sell everything from French perfumes and Swiss watches to Japanese cameras and Irish linen.
W Atlantic Drive, at W Sunrise Hwy.
Open: Mon–Sat 9am–6pm.

Port Lucaya Marketplace

This $10-million, 2.5ha (6-acre) site is Grand Bahama's latest shopping, dining and entertainment complex, and these days a far busier spot than the International Bazaar.

It overlooks a busy marina, and there are several good value cafés among the T-shirt stores and boutiques.

If you fancy investigating marine life in the colourful coral reefs without getting your hair wet, get on to one of the glass-bottomed boats that make regular departures from the port; the Lucaya Beach is across the road.
Royal Palm Way. Open: Mon–Sat 9am–6pm.

NEW PROVIDENCE

Measuring just 11km by 34km (7 miles by 21 miles), New Providence became the chief Bahamanian island by virtue of its north coast harbour, site of present-day Nassau. This was the seat of the British administration until independence in 1973, and there is still a rather sleepy Anglo influence in historic Nassau, with its pith-helmeted policemen, horse-drawn carriages and shady squares.

Arrival

Ships dock at one of the three piers King George's Wharf, right on Nassau Harbour and close to busy Rawson Square; from the dock, you can easily explore the town on foot. However, you'll need a car to get to Paradise Island, Cable Beach and other attractions. Taxis line up to meet the ships just outside the port, and fares are set by the government.

Ardastra Gardens and Conservation Centre

Set in 2ha (5 acres) of tropical gardens, the Centre is home to around 300 birds and beasts from parrots, meerkats and ocelots to a troupe of marching flamingoes, the Bahamas' national bird.
2.5km (1½ miles) west of Nassau via Chippingham Rd. Tel: (242) 323 5806; www.ardastra.com. Open: daily 9am–5pm. Admission charge.

Cable Beach

This popular and busy 6.5km (4-mile) white-sand beach, known as the 'Bahamanian Riviera', fronts the island's biggest and best resort hotels, such as the 1,550-room Wyndham Nassau

JUNKANOO

Cultural highlight of the Bahamanian year, the Junkanoo carnival kicks off on Boxing Day with a 'rush' (parade) through the streets of Nassau and Grand Bahama's West End. Costumed masquerades, decorated floats, dancers and bands are urged on by drums, whistles and home-made noisemakers in a national celebration with tangible African roots. The party atmosphere, beauty pageants and competitions climax in the New Year's Day Parade, but visitors can get a taste of Junkanoo year-round at the **Junkanoo Expo**, Prince George Dock, in Nassau, New Providence. *Open: daily 9am–5.30pm.*

Resort and Crystal Palace Casino. You'll find watersports galore, glass-bottomed boat trips and fine dining opportunities.
5km (3 miles) west of Nassau via West Bay St.

Fort Charlotte

Built to guard Nassau Harbour at the end of the 18th century, this sprawling, low-slung fortress affords grand views from its hilltop site. Above the moat, the white stone battlements are reinforced with cannons, while below ground you can visit the dungeons, complete with medieval-looking torture devices. Grafted on to the hillside below Fort Charlotte, Nassau's Botanical Gardens offer a cat's cradle of paths, steps and leafy bowers.
Off West Bay St, 1.6km (1 mile) west of Nassau. Tel: (242) 325 9186. Open: daily 8am–4.30pm. Admission charge.

Nassau

Lined with historic buildings, Rawson Square is a bustling spot and a centre for the annual Junkanoo celebrations. On the west side of the square, there are horse-drawn surreys for hire. The chatty drivers provide 45-minute tours for two. Across Bay Street, Nassau's main thoroughfare and shopping district, the pink-and-white House of Assembly faces Parliament Square (starting point for the Nassau Walk (*see pp60–61*). Cheap and frequent minibus services to Cable Beach leave from Bay Street and ferries make regular crossings to Paradise Island.

Paradise Island

Known as Hog Island until 1962, the developer of this small island, linked to Nassau by a toll causeway (nominal charge for pedestrians), decided a name change was necessary in order to attract tourists. There are fine beaches to the west and to the north, exclusive hotels such as Disney's massive Atlantis resort, with its excellent water park – non-guests can buy day-passes. The resort also holds Dolphin Cay, where you can swim with dolphins. On Paradise Island Drive, near the deluxe Ocean Club, is the pretty Versailles Gardens and French Cloister. The elegant 14th-century cloister, with its slim columns and carved capitals, was brought from the famous French pilgrimage town of Lourdes.

Paradise Island is just off the northeast coast of Nassau, reached by a toll bridge from Nassau. The bridge is walkable, and you can also get there by jitney bus from Bay Street, ferry from Prince George Wharf (*daily 9am–6pm*), or by water taxi.
Atlantis Resort. Tel: (242) 363 3000; www.atlantis.com

The Yacht Harbour in Nassau

Walk: Nassau

Behind the busy port, which can handle up to ten cruise liners per day, Nassau's compact old town climbs uphill from the waterfront. It is easily explored on foot, and this relaxed walk combines a stroll down bustling Bay Street with visits to a small selection of historic sites.

Allow 2 hours.

Start at Parliament Square.

1 Parliament Square

The traditional hub of Bahamanian government, three sides of the square are bordered by the colonial-style, pink-painted buildings of the House of Assembly, the Ministry of Finance and the Supreme Court. In front sits a statue of an uncharacteristically young Queen Victoria flanked by cannons.

Head west (left) along Bay St.

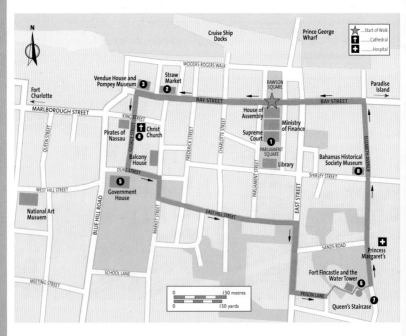

2 Straw Market

A visitor favourite for years, Straw Market houses almost 500 craft vendors under a 2,800sq m (30,000sq ft) canvas structure – light, airy and brimming with bargains.

Continue west along Bay St.

3 Vendue House and Pompey Museum

Slave auctions were once held in this 18th-century building facing George Street. Today, the museum displays Bahamanian history exhibits and paintings by folk artist Amos Ferguson. These naïve renderings of colourful local scenes are now collectors' items.

Open: Mon–Wed & Fri–Sat 9.30am–4.30pm, Sun 9.30am–12.30pm, closed Thur. Admission charge. Walk up George St to the corner of King St.

4 Christ Church Cathedral

Built on the site of the first church in the Bahamas, the graceful interior of the 18th- to 19th-century cathedral is lined with tall windows to catch the breeze. Wall plaques bear testament to a history of fevers and shipwrecks.

Continue up George St to Duke St.

5 Government House

The Governor-General's imposing residence sits at the top of shady George Street, clad in the official pink-and-white Bahamanian colour scheme. A statue of Christopher Columbus strikes a rakish pose on the steps.

Walk east (right) on Duke St and then turn right on Market St and take the steps up to East Hill, site of the blue-painted Friendship sculpture, given by the people of Mexico. Turn left along East Hill St, right on East St, then turn left up Prison Lane.

6 Fort Fincastle and the Water Tower

Dating from 1793, the fortress with its sharp-nosed prow never actually fired a shot in anger. It was, however, a useful lighthouse and signal station. Climb up on to the cannon-lined turret and sloping 'deck' for views of the harbour. For a real panorama, take a trip up the 38m (126ft) Water Tower.

Open: daily 8am–5pm. Free admission.

7 Queen's Staircase

Take the 66-step staircase down to Princess Margaret's Hospital and Elizabeth Avenue. The staircase was carved out of the limestone hillside by slave labour in the 18th century.

Walk left down Elizabeth Ave towards Bay St.

8 Bahamas Historical Society Museum

This modest Bahamas Historical Society Museum charts local history with the aid of period maps, paintings and photographs.

Tel: (242) 322 4231.
www.bahamashistoricalsociety.com.
Open: Mon, Tue, Thur & Fri 10am–4pm, Sat 10am–noon.
Admission charge.

Barbados

A pear-shaped island measuring 23km by 34km (15 miles by 22 miles), Barbados lies around 150km (100 miles) east of the Windward island chain. It was noticed, but not settled, by early Spanish and Portuguese adventurers who named the island Los Barbudos, or 'the bearded ones', after its native banyan (ficus) trees, which drop a curtain of aerial roots towards the ground.

Barbados was uninhabited when the British claimed it in 1625, though its favourable climate and rich soil were to make it one of the most successful colonies in the West Indies. The British ruled for more than 300 uninterrupted years until independence in 1966, and signs of their influence still linger on. Familiar place names abound, from Bridgetown's Trafalgar Square to the hilly Scotland district in the northeast. The national sport (and abiding passion) is cricket, and there is even a touch of a West Country accent in the lilting Bajan speech.

There is plenty to see and do around the island; the sights are spread out around the various districts, typically named after saints. The sheltered west coast is famous for its smart hotels and seamless strip of white sand; the surf-lashed and rocky east coast is more picturesque, but swimming is dangerous.

Arrival

Barbados' swish cruise ship dock is at the Deep Water Harbour in Carlisle Bay, close to Bridgetown in the island's southwest. From the dock, it's a fifteen-minute walk into the capital – just follow the shoreline south along the Careenage. Taxis also line up to make the short hop into town or to take tourists to the island's many attractions and beaches. Taxis are unmetred, but rates are set by the government. The bus service in Barbados is reliable, and also connects the port with Bridgetown, from where you can get services to most points on the island.

Barbados Tourism Authority

PO Box 242, (Harbour Road), Bridgetown.
Tel: (246) 427 2623.
Also see: www.barbados.org
There is also a pierside information kiosk.

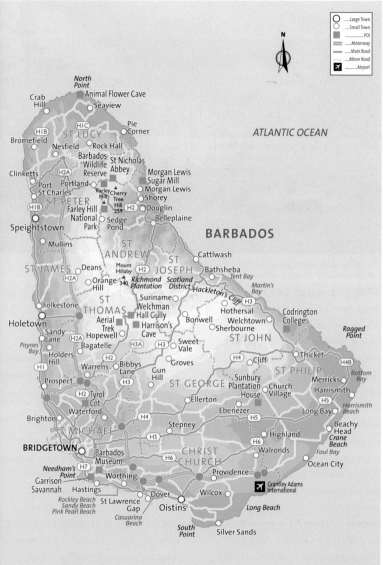

Barbados

- Large Town
- Small Town
- POI
- Motorway
- Main Road
- Minor Road
- ✈ Airport

N

ATLANTIC OCEAN

North Point
Animal Flower Cave
Crab Hill
Seaview
Pie Corner
H1B
H1C
ST LUCY
Bromefield
Nesfield
Rock Hall
Clinketts
H2A
Barbados Wildlife Reserve
St Nicholas Abbey
Morgan Lewis Sugar Mill
Port St Charles
Portland
Farley Hill
Cherry Tree Hill 259
Morgan Lewis
Shorey
H1B
ST PETER
Farley Hill National Park
H2
Douglin
Belleplaine
Speightstown
Sedge Pond
Mullins
ST ANDREW
BARBADOS
Cattlwash
ST JAMES
Deans
Mount Hillaby
H2
ST JOSEPH
Bathsheba
Tent Bay
H2A
Orange Hill
340
Richmond Plantation
Scotland District
Hackleton's Cliff
Martin's Bay
Folkestone
ST THOMAS
Suriname
Welchman Hall Gully
H3
Holetown
Aerial Trek
Hothersal
Codrington College
Ragged Point
Sandy Lane
Hopewell
Harrison's Cave
Bonwell
Welchtown
Sherbourne
H2A
Paynes Bay
Bagatelle
H3A
H3
Sweet Vale
ST JOHN
Holders Hill
H1
H2
Bibbys Lane
Groves
H4
Cliff
Thicket
H4B
Warrens
Gun Hill
Sunbury Plantation House
Merricks
Bottom Bay
Prospect
H3
ST GEORGE
Church Village
Harrismith
H2
Tyrol Cot
Ellerton
H5
Harrismith Beach
Waterford
H4
Ebenezer
H5
Long Bay
Brighton
Stepney
Beachy Head
ST MICHAEL
H5
Highland
Crane Beach
BRIDGETOWN
Barbados Museum
H6
Walronds
Foul Bay
Needham's Point
H7
CHRIST CHURCH
H6
Providence
Ocean City
Garrison Savannah
Worthing
Hastings
Wilcox
Grantley Adams International
Rockley Beach
Sandy Beach
Pink Pearl Beach
St Lawrence Gap
Dover
Oistins
Long Beach
Casuarina Beach
South Point
Silver Sands

Caribbean Sea

0   2km
0   1 mile

The Promenade in Bridgetown

Bridgetown and environs

More than a third of the island's total population of 254,000 live in the capital, Bridgetown. This bustling town pivots around central National Heroes (formerly Trafalgar) Square, overlooked by a statue of Lord Nelson erected in 1813 – (more than two decades ahead of its counterpart in London). Off the square is Broad Street, the main commercial thoroughfare, with legions of duty-free stores. To the north, part of the mellow stone Public Buildings complex is occupied by the House of Assembly. Though the site only dates from the 19th century, the Bajan parliament is the third oldest in the Commonwealth (after Britain and Bermuda), founded in 1639. A short walk east, 18th-century St Michael's Cathedral was rebuilt on the site of the original mid-17th century church. To the south of the square, the Chamberlain Bridge crosses the Careenage (a finger of sea) to a handful of pleasant cafés facing the waterfront.

Andromeda Gardens

This beautiful 2.5ha (6-acre) garden, perched on the east coast cliffs with glimpses of the bay below, was founded in 1954. Today, it is world-renowned for its variety of exotic species – orchids, heliconia, hibiscus, palms and cacti; and there are arches bound with fragrant stephanotis, frangipani trees and clouds of multicoloured bougainvillea. Shaded corners reveal a mass of ferns and marvellous ornamental foliage.

Bathsheba, 16km (10 miles) northeast of Bridgetown. Tel: (246) 433 9384; andromeda.cavehill.uwi.edu. Open: daily 9am–5pm. Admission charge.

Animal Flower Cave

Twenty-seven deep steps lead down to this underground cave in the cliffs. Paddle about among the stalactites and stalagmites with a guide and watch yellow, orange and green sea anemones that gave the cave its name wave their tiny tentacles in the rock pools. There is also a swimming hole.

North Point, 8 St Lucy District, 25km (17 miles) north of Bridgetown. Tel: (246) 439 8797. Open: daily 9am–6pm. Admission charge.

Barbados Museum

Laid out in the old military prison, which formed part of the British garrison, this museum traces Bajan history through the ages. Collections of Amerindian artefacts, military memorabilia and exhibits relating to sugar production and Africans in Barbados are displayed in a series of old cells. There are also antique maps, portraits and photographs, a children's section, natural history displays and a fine art gallery.

St Anne's Garrison, 1.5km (1 mile) south of Bridgetown. Tel: (246) 427 0201; www.barbmuse.org.bb. Open: Mon–Sat 9am–5pm, Sun 2–6pm. Admission charge.

Garrison Savannah

Once a British army parade ground, Garrison Savannah is now home to the Barbados Turf Club. Twenty race meetings a year take place on Saturdays on the grassy course, which is also popular with joggers. Around the Savannah there is an interesting collection of 19th-century British-built buildings, old barracks, and rampart ruins belonging to Charles Fort (built in the 17th century) and St Anne's Fort, begun in 1704 but never completed.

The distinctive red-painted Main Guard (also known as the Savannah Club) is being restored to house a reception centre, although there's not much to see inside.

Off Garrison Hill (2.5km/1½ miles south of Bridgetown).

Barbados

Three hundred years ago around 500 cane-crushing windmills existed in Barbados

Northern Barbados
Barbados Wildlife Reserve

Set in 1.6ha (4 acres) of natural mahogany forest, this reserve provides a safe haven for green monkeys, or vervets, considered a pest by local farmers. Brick paths through the woods offer a chance to spot Brocket deer, lumbering tortoises, porcupines, agoutis and playful otters. There is also a walk-through aviary, reptile cages and a caiman pool, where these alligator-like creatures bask on the sunny banks. Pleasantly shaded, well-signposted nature trails in the adjacent Grenade Hall Forest provide an introduction to the local flora.
Farley Hill, St Peter District, 18km (12 miles) north of Bridgetown. Tel: (246) 422 8826. www.barbados.org/reserve.htm. Open: daily 10am–5pm. Admission charge.

Farley Hill National Park and Wildlife Reserve

A good spot to relax with a picnic, this national park is perched on a 274m (900ft) cliff with views over the rugged Scotland district. Laid out around the ruins of a 19th-century plantation house, the lovely landscaped grounds are planted with a wide variety of trees.

The unusual gabled façade of 17th-century St Nicholas Abbey

St Peter District, 17km (11 miles) north of Bridgetown. Tel: (246) 422 3555. Open: daily 7am–6pm. Admission charge for vehicles.

Morgan Lewis Sugar Mill

This 250-year-old sugar-grinding mill is the largest surviving windmill in the Caribbean region, complete with restored machinery and sails. It was in commercial use right up until 1944 (and is still in full working order), and affords panoramic views over the surrounding countryside.
St Andrew District, 18km (12 miles) north of Bridgetown. Tel: (246) 426 2421. Open: Mon–Sat 9am–5pm. Admission charge.

St Nicholas Abbey

A gabled manor house built around 1650 to 1660, the 'abbey' is a rare example of Jacobean architecture in the Caribbean, and one of only three in the entire Americas. The ground floor is lined with panelled walls (an old trick for concealing damp blisters in the tropics) and has been carefully restored.
St Peter District, 18km (12 miles) north of Bridgetown. Tel: (246) 422 8725; www.stnicholasabbey.com. Open: Mon–Fri 10am–3.30pm. Admission charge.

Central Barbados
Harrison's Cave

This magnificent cave system, one of Barbados' most popular attractions, stretches 2.3km (1½ miles) and is packed

with stalagmites and stalagtites and networked by streams. Visitors are taken through on a tram, with guides pointing out different features and giving you the lowdown on cave systems.
St Thomas District, 7km (4¼ miles) northeast of Bridgetown. Tel: (246) 438 6640; www.harrisonscave.com. Open: daily 9am–4pm. Admission charge.

Welchman Hall Gully

A favourite with plant lovers, this lush wooded gully was first laid out as a botanical walk in the 1860s. Abandoned for many years, it was rescued by the Barbados National Trust in 1962, and restored to a cool forest habitat with a 1.5km (1 mile) long path edged by towering bamboo, palms, nutmeg, clove and fig trees. Families of green monkeys crash about overhead in the late afternoon.
St Joseph District, 10km (7 miles) northeast of Bridgetown. Tel: (246) 438 6671; www.welchmanhallgullybarbados.com. Open: daily 9am–4.30pm. Admission charge.

Eastern Barbados

Codrington College

A magnificent driveway lined with lofty cabbage palms leads down to the elegant façade of this Anglican theological college, the oldest in the Western hemisphere. It was founded in 1745 and named after its benefactor, Christopher Codrington, a governor

---

> ### HISTORIC BUILDINGS
> In addition to St Nicholas Abbey and the Sunbury Plantation House, Barbados has another notable historic home. **Tyrol Cot**, just north of Bridgetown, was home to two former prime ministers of Barbados, Sir Grantley Adams and his son, Tom. Today it is the centre of the island's heritage museum; other dwellings include a chattel house and a rum shop (*Tel: (246) 424 2074. Open: Mon–Fri 9am–5pm. Admission charge*).

of the Leeward Islands, who was brought up in the original Codrington mansion, now the Principal's Lodge.
St John District, 17km (11 miles) northeast of Bridgetown. Tel: (246) 423 1140. Open: daily 10am–4pm. Admission charge.

Sunbury Plantation House

This comfortable 300-year-old plantation house first appears on a map dated 1681, and was a family home until 1985. It has survived several major hurricanes thanks to its sturdy 76cm (2½ft) thick walls. Fresh flowers and pot plants add a homely air to the reception rooms which contain mahogany furniture, antique silver and glassware, tall hurricane lamps and 19th-century engravings. Upstairs, there are displays of Victorian clothing laid out on four-poster beds. An old yam cellar houses agricultural artefacts, domestic utensils and a cart and carriage museum.
St Philip District, 15km (9¼ miles) east of Bridgetown. Tel: (246) 423 6270; www.barbadosgreathouse.com. Open: daily 9am–5pm. Admission charge.

Bermuda

The Bermuda Islands, Britain's oldest colony and spiritual home of the ubiquitous knee-length shorts introduced by the British military around the beginning of the 20th century, lie about 1,050km (650 miles) east of Cape Hatteras, North Carolina, in the Atlantic Ocean. Warmed by the Gulf Stream and protected by the world's most northerly coral reefs, seven of the 150 islands are connected by bridges and causeways to form Bermuda, where cruise ships dock at three different ports.

The islands were discovered by Spanish explorer Juan Bermúdez in 1503, but settled only in the early 17th century by the British, after Sir George Somers was shipwrecked off St George's Island in 1609. Today, Bermuda is a popular summer season destination, delightfully British, with pubs and cricket pitches, luxuriant gardens and pretty pastel-painted cottages. It also tends to be the only port of call which allows passengers a full three or four days for exploring.

Visitors Service Bureau

There are visitor information bureaus at all three cruise ship ports. In Hamilton, it's at *69 Front Street, tel: (441) 536 4636.* In St George, it's just off *Water Street Plaza, tel: (441) 297 8000;* and at the Royal Naval Dockyard, it's at *Pier 41, Clocktower Parade, tel: (441) 799 4842. For more infomation about Bermuda also see: www.bermudatourism.com*

Arrival

Bermuda has three cruise-ship docks. The dock at Hamilton (the capital) is right in the city itself, with the wharf on Hamilton's main thoroughfare, Front Street. You can see Hamilton on foot, but taxis line up along the front. St George's dock also allows ships to moor up right in the heart of St George, with the dock located on Ordnance Island, a short stroll from the centre. Again, taxis are available for

THE BERMUDA RAILWAY TRAIL

Once upon a time visitors to Bermuda would have been able to 'rattle and shake' from one end of the island to the other by train. Taken out of service 30 years ago, the old railroad has been given a new lease of life as the Bermuda Railway Trail, and offers a lovely way of taking in some of the island's scenery. Pick up a free guide to the trail from the tourist office. It is broken up into easy-to-walk sections of around 3km (2 miles), and there is access from numerous points around the island, including Hamilton.

excursions. Right at the western end of the island, the Royal Naval Dockyard is a little farther from the action, but taxis are plentiful and buses also run to most points around Bermuda. All taxis are metered, with fares regulated by the government. Note that car rental is not allowed in Bermuda.

Bermuda Aquarium, Museum and Zoo

The Bermuda Aquarium, Museum and Zoo (BAMZ) offers a fascinating insight into the subtropical and tropical marine world. You'll find an amazing collection of brilliantly coloured sea creatures, from tiny fish and seahorses to penguins, seals and Galapágos turtles, plus a natural

history museum, and a Zoological Garden with a screeching, dazzling, entertaining collection of tropical birds and animals.

40 North Shore Rd, Harrington Sound.
Tel: (441) 293 2727; www.bamz.org.
Open: daily 9am–5pm.
Admission charge.

Bermuda Arts Centre and Craft Market

The Arts Centre occupies the former cooperage building, providing a display area for contemporary arts and crafts and travelling shows. You can watch the six resident artists at work, and buy souvenirs such as handblown glass, quilts, pottery and prints of Bermudan scenes.

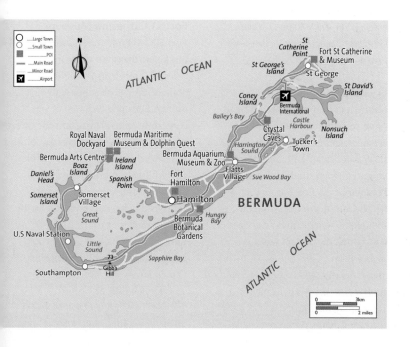

Arts Centre. Tel: (441) 234 2809;
www.artbermuda.bm. Open: daily
10am–5pm.
Craft Market. Tel: (441) 234 3208.
Open: daily 9.30am–6pm.
Free admission.

Bermuda Botanical Gardens (Camden)

Camden, the Bermuda premier's
official residence, is set in these 14.5ha
(36-acre) botanical gardens, founded in
1898. As well as formally planted areas
and an aromatic garden for visually
impaired visitors, there are subtropical
fruit groves, rare Bermuda cedars,
banyan trees, a kitchen garden, an
orchid house and an aviary.
169 South Rd, Paget (east of Hamilton).
Tel: (441) 236 4201. Visitors Centre.
Open: Mon–Fri 9.30am–3.30pm.
Gardens. Open: daily sunrise–sunset.
Free admission.

Crystal Caves

Nature is at its most bizarre in these
subterranean caves. Fantastic
arrangements of stalactites and
stalagmites create an eerie landscape
around underground saltwater lagoons.
Pontoon bridges edge around the pools,
which reach depths of 17m (55ft),
though the water is so crystal-clear
you'd think the bottom was just
inches away.
Wilkinson Ave, off Harrington Sound Rd,
Baileys Bay. Tel: (441) 293 0640;
www.caves.bm. Open: Apr–Oct daily
9.30am–4.30pm. Admission charge.

THE BERMUDA TRIANGLE

A triangular patch of the Atlantic Ocean
bounded by Bermuda, Florida and Puerto
Rico, the Bermuda Triangle is the legendary
graveyard for dozens of boats and planes, lost
without trace. At least 100 ships and 1,000
sailors disappeared in the region during the
latter part of the 20th century. One of the
strangest incidents was the disappearance of
five US torpedo bombers that took off on a
routine two-hour patrol from Fort
Lauderdale on 5 December 1945. Just before
they were due to return, the patrol leader was
asked to describe his position and replied,
'We don't know which way west is. Everything
is wrong … even the ocean doesn't look as
it should.' After radio contact was lost a
search plane went out – it also disappeared.
The US Navy commenced a five-year study,
Project Magnet, to investigate the possibility
of magnetic interference. Nothing was
ever proved.

Fort St Catherine Museum

Fort St Catherine was founded in 1614
on the northeastern tip of the islands,
where the survivors of Sir George
Somers' shipwreck supposedly first set
foot on Bermuda (see p68). It was
constantly refortified against the threat
of an invasion (which never came), and
has battlements 8m (25ft) thick, plus
powerful 18-ton muzzle-loading
cannons. Inside there are recently
revamped historical displays, plus an
audio-visual tour of the islands'
military outposts, a recreated cook
house and replicas of the British
Crown Jewels.
15 Coot Pond Rd, St George.
Tel: (441) 297 1920. Open: Mon–Fri
10am–4pm. Admission charge.

Hamilton

Bermuda's main cruise port and capital, Hamilton is a top shopping spot and an excellent base for trips around the island. When you want to take a break from shopping there are several attractions to visit. On Church Street is the 19th-century **Bermuda Cathedral**. Close by, on the same street, **Bermuda National Gallery**'s collections of 15th-to 19th-century oil paintings and watercolours, alongside temporary exhibits, are housed in the modern **City Hall** (*Tel: (441) 295 9428; www.bermudanationalgallery.com. Open: Mon–Fri 10am–4pm, Sat 10am–2pm. Admission charge*). On Parliament Street, off Front Street, on weekdays you can also visit the Sessions House (or Supreme Court), seat of the second oldest parliament in the world. A short walk west of Front Street brings you to Par-la-Ville Gardens and the Perot Post Office on Queen Street. Here you will find the **Historical Society Museum** with its eclectic collection of antiques and colonial memorabilia *Tel: (441) 295 2487. Open: Mon–Sat 9.30am–3.30pm. Free admission*).

Fort Hamilton

East of the city centre, Fort Hamilton, complete with moat and winding underground passages, affords a panoramic view of the town and harbour.
Off Happy Valley Rd. Tel: (441) 292 1234. Open: daily 9.30am–5pm. Free admission.

Maritime Museum

Housed in the old military buildings of the Keep Citadel, this interesting and informative museum illustrates Bermuda's long and colourful maritime history, from whaling and shipbuilding to piracy and rum-running. There are intricate model ships and nautical knick-knacks, gold and artefacts salvaged from wrecks displayed in the well-stocked Treasure House. You can also swim with dolphins at the **Dolphin Quest** attraction within the museum grounds.
Tel: (441) 234 1418; www.bmm.bm. Open: daily 9.30am–5pm. Admission charge. Dolphin Quest. Tel: (441) 234 4464; www.dolphinquest.org. Open: daily 9.30am–4.30pm.

Royal Naval Dockyard

The naval dockyard was developed in the 19th century, inspired by the Duke of Wellington's vision that Bermuda should become the 'Gibraltar of the West'. Heavily fortified and equipped with numerous ordnance buildings, barracks and a cooperage, the yard also boasts a splendid 30m (100ft) high clock tower, and the world's largest floating dry dock. The dockyard's new role is as a shopping, sightseeing, dining and nightlife complex.
Royal Naval Dockyard is 24km (15 miles) northwest of Hamilton. Ferries (30-minute journey time) depart from Hamilton, and there are efficient bus services.

Walk: St George

This picturesque port was the original capital of Bermuda (transferred to Hamilton in 1815), and has been immaculately preserved. It was designated a World Heritage Site by UNESCO in 2000.

Allow 2–3 hours.

Start at the replica of Deliverance.

1 Replica of *Deliverance*

This tub-like vessel is a faithful replica of the 17th-century ship, one of two sailing ships built by Sir George Somers' crew (*see p68*) in order to

continue their journey to America. *Cross the bridge to King's Square.*

2 Town Hall

The Town Hall is home to the 'Bermuda Journey' multimedia presentation.

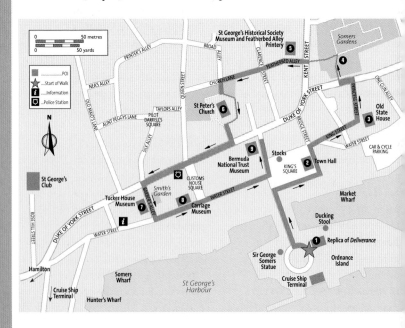

Open: Mon–Sat 10am–4pm. Free admission.
From the top right-hand corner of the square, head east (right) on King St.

3 Old State House

The Old State House was built in the Italian fashion by Governor Nathaniel Butler – who believed Bermuda was on the same latitude as Italy. It's now in use as a Masonic Lodge.
Open: most Weds 10am–3pm.
Free admission.
Walk north on Princess St.

4 Somers Gardens

Here lies buried the heart of Sir George Somers, who bravely sailed back to Bermuda from Jamestown, Virginia, to find supplies for the beleaguered colonists.
Cross Kent St to Featherbed Alley.

5 St George's Historical Society Museum and Featherbed Alley Printery

The Historical Museum, housed in a typical 18th-century Bermudan cottage, depicts bygone island life. Just around the corner, the Printery contains an antique press.
St George's Historical Society Museum.
Open: Mon–Fri 10am–4pm.
Joint admission charge with Printery.
Featherbed Alley Printery.
Open: Mon–Fri 10am–4pm.
Head west across Clarence St on to Church Lane.

6 St Peter's Church

Take a good look around the gravestones (some are over 300 years old), before entering the church, built in 1713. The church treasure is displayed in the vestry.
Exit right on to Duke of York St, cross Queen St, turn left into Barber's Alley.

7 Tucker House Museum

Once home to one of Bermuda's most important families, this fine historic house is furnished with collections of cedar furniture, oil paintings, silver and antiques.
Open: Mon–Sat 10am–4pm, closed Mon & Tues Nov–March. Admission charge.
Turn left (east) into Water St.

8 Carriage Museum

The first automobiles didn't arrive in Bermuda until 1946 so, until then, Bermudans got around in a variety of horse-drawn carriages.
Open: Mon–Fri 10am–4pm. Admission by donation.
Head east on Water St towards King's Square and turn left to return to Duke of York St.

9 Bermuda National Trust Museum

Island history exhibits include an interesting section on Bermuda's role in the American Civil War. The island was a vital staging post for Confederate blockade runners involved in forwarding arms from Europe to the Confederacy.
Open: Mon–Sat 10am–4pm.
Admission charge.

Cayman Islands

Now famous for offshore banking, diving and tax-free shopping, these low coral islands are in fact the summits of underwater mountains and were spotted by Christopher Columbus on his fourth voyage in 1503. He named them Las Tortugas, 'the turtles', for their once abundant turtle population. The name did not stick, however, and the islands were rechristened Las Caymanas after the Carib Indian word for crocodiles.

The islands were ceded to Britain (together with Jamaica) in the Treaty of Madrid (1670) and were governed in tandem with the larger island. When Jamaica claimed independence in 1962, the Caymans chose to become a British Crown Colony. The largest and southernmost island of the group is Grand Cayman, home to around 26,000 of the 28,000 Caymanians. The rest live on the little sister islands of Cayman Brac and Little Cayman to the northeast.

Arrival

Ships dock just offshore of George Town, and tenders transport passengers to the Harbour Drive pier, which is right in the middle of the shopping district and within walking distance of Seven Mile Beach.

GRAND CAYMAN

An ever-popular stop with the cruising fraternity, Grand Cayman is relaxed, well-organised and virtually free of crime.

It is easy to get around, with local buses as well as taxis plying the northbound road from George Town, past the alluring white sand expanse of Seven Mile Beach to West Bay and covering the island's main attractions along the way.

George Town

As you step ashore at George Town, the tourist information booth offers helpful information and maps, including a *Historic Walking Tour* of the town. The main shopping areas are around Fort Street and the Kirk Freeport Plaza, but you might also want to check out the National Gallery, which stages exhibitions of works by local and international artists inspired by the islands.

National Gallery. Harbour Place.
Tel: (345) 945 8111;
ww.nationalgallery.org.ky.
Open: Mon–Fri 9am–5pm, Sat 11am–4pm.
Free admission.

Cayman Islands National Museum

Located in the Old Courthouse and Jail, this museum houses a fine range of exhibits charting the island's turbulent history of pirates and wreckers.

Harbour Drive, at Shedden Rd.
Tel: (345) 949 8368; www.museum.ky.
Open: Mon–Fri 9am–5pm,
Sat 9am–1pm. Admission charge.

Boatswain's Beach

Popular marine park that houses everything from a huge pool and snorkelling lagoon to a 'Predators' Reef' aquarium with daily shark feeding; it also encompasses the world's only commercial green turtle farm, which plays a conservation role by releasing a small percentage of its captive-bred turtles back into the wild. Here you'll find thousands of turtles in varying stages of development, from incubating eggs to 270kg (600lb) monsters, and you can pet them in the touch-tanks. Hard-hearted visitors can sample traditional Cayman turtle dishes in the café. (NB: Turtle products cannot be imported into the USA or UK.)

West Bay Rd. Tel: (345) 949 3894;
www.boatswainsbeach.ky. Open:
Mon–Thur 8.30am–4.30pm, Fri–Sun
8.30am–10pm. Admission charge.

Hell

A well-trodden path, the road to Hell, ends up in a touristy spread of gift shops and T-shirt sellers. The weathered outcrop of ironstone here is

Grand Cayman

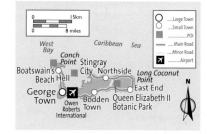

more than 1½ million years old.
West Bay Rd, West Bay.

Stingray City

Touted as 'the best 12-foot dive in the world', this extraordinary dive and snorkel site brings its many visitors within petting distance of stingrays, some of which measure 1.8m (6ft) from wingtip to wingtip. For those wary of entering the water, boats allow passengers to at least watch the graceful creatures in the gin-clear sea.

Queen Elizabeth II Botanic Park

Opened by its regal namesake in 1994, the Queen Elizabeth II Botanic Park features a well-marked woodland trail, swamp area, habitat for the endangered blue iguana habitat and ponds for freshwater turtles, as well as more than 200 plant species and a Heritage Garden that recreates traditional homes.

Frank Sound Rd, North Side, around
25km (15 miles) northeast of George
Town. Tel: (345) 947 9462;
www.botanic-park.ky. Open: Oct–March
9am–5.30pm, April–Sept 9am–6.30pm.
Admission charge.

Underwater world

'Ah, but you should be here at Carnival time,' they say. The brilliant colours, the swirling costumes, the pretty girls and vaguely sinister folkloric figures lend an exotic air to the Caribbean scene. Well, it is Carnival time every day of the year just below the surface of the glassy azure sea. The Caribbean region offers some of the most magnificent underwater scenery in the world, and it is yours for the price of a snorkel. In fact, you don't even have to get your feet wet, as flotillas of glass-bottomed boats and mini-submarines ferry visitors out over the reefs to view the colourful spectacle below.

Coral reefs are living entities built by limestone-secreting polyps. The forests of staghorn and elkhorn corals, delicate sea fans, feathers and whips of soft coral provide a fantastic backdrop for all manner of cute and bizarre sea creatures. Darting electric blue kissing fish (chromis), rock beauties, elegant grey angelfish and busy shoals of their black-and-yellow striped cousins, the sergeant majors, patrol beneath the waves. Sharp-beaked parrot fish crunch thoughtfully on chunks of hard coral, extracting the polyps and algae, while evil-looking eels lurk in crevices, their beady eyes also on the lookout for lunch. Decorator crabs – so-called for their habit of adorning their shells with an eclectic array of camouflage materials – scramble around the rocks surrounded by starfish, sea urchins and lobsters.

Top dive spots in the Caribbean include Aruba, Bonaire and Curaçao

Inquisitive sharks and brilliant queen angelfish

Petrified forests of delicate coral are part of the scenery beneath the waves

(with a 5ha/12-acre underwater park), both in the Netherlands Antilles; reef and wreck sites in the Virgin Islands; the Bahamas; off Antigua; Barbados; Dominica; St Lucia; and the French island of Martinique. Probably the most spectacular diving of all is in the Cayman Islands, where the famous Cayman Wall plummets 6,000m (20,000ft) straight down to the seabed. Grand Cayman's other claim to fame is 'Stingray City' in the sheltered waters of the North Sound, where divers and snorkellers can experience close encounters with huge, semi-tame stingrays (see p75).

POPULAR DIVE SPOTS

ABC Islands – the Dutch Leeward Islands of Aruba, Bonaire and Curaçao (the latter features a 5ha (12-acre) underwater park) have many excellent sites.

Bahamas – the reef off Andros is spectacular.

British Virgin Islands – the wreck of the RMS *Rhone*, off Tortola, is arguably the best wreck dive in the Caribbean.

Cayman Islands – possibly the best scuba diving in the Caribbean. Swim with huge, semi-tame stingrays at Stingray City, or experience the 'north wall'.

Turks and Caicos – these islands are just opening up to scuba diving, with many new and colourful 'virgin' sites still being discovered.

Dominica

The 'Nature Island of the Caribbean', Dominica (pronounced Dom-in-eek-a) is lush, green, mountainous and, almost invariably, wet. The Carib Indians called it Wai'tukubuli, meaning 'tall is her body', and Dominica's soaring interior scrambles up to a peak of 1,400m (4,500ft) from a base that measures just 47km by 26km (29 by 16 miles).

It is said that of all the Caribbean islands, Christopher Columbus would have least trouble recognising Dominica as it has changed so little. He landed here on 3 November 1493, a Sunday, hence its name. The warlike Carib inhabitants discouraged early European settlers and the wild jungle interior became a sanctuary for runaway slaves and for Caribs flushed from other islands by the colonists. Despite a controlling British influence from 1763 until independence in 1978, Dominica retains few reminders of its former colonial masters. English may be the island's official language, but most of the locals speak French patois.

It has always been hard to make a living on Dominica, so the island has remained largely unspoiled– a boon for the makers of the *Pirates of the Caribbean* movies, who filmed numerous scenes here. The island's lack of development has aided the survival of the Carib people, too, once widespread throughout the Caribbean,

and is also a trump card in courting the ecotourism market. The island's Northern Forest Reserve is an important refuge for two endangered parrot species. The 50cm (20in) tall

Sisserou (Imperial Parrot) is one of the largest Amazon parrots, with mainly green plumage and deep purple breast feathers; its more colourful cousin, the Jaco (red-necked parrot), is distinguished by a tell-tale flash of scarlet at its throat.

Dominica Division of Tourism
Bay Front, Roseau. Tel: (767) 448 2045. Also see: www.dominica.dm

Arrival

Most cruise ships dock at the ferry terminal on the Bayfront in Roseau, from where you can explore the town on foot. Some vessels also dock at Portsmouth adjacent to the Cabrits National Park. At both docks, taxis (often minibuses) line up to meet ships in port, but as fares are unmetered, it's important to agree on a price before getting in.

Roseau

The island capital, Roseau, reaches south of the Roseau River mouth in a grid of busy streets lined with weather-beaten wooden buildings. Sagging balconies, peeling gingerbread features and rusty tin roofs give it a faded charm, but there is plenty of life in the open-air market by the river.

Opposite the cruise ship dock on the Bayfront, the Dominica Museum gives some basic background on the island's history. Behind the museum is the old cobbled market, **Dawbiney Place**, set back from the waterfront off King George V Street, with stalls selling souvenirs.

A saleswoman proudly displays her wares at Roseau market

The 19th-century stone **Cathedral of the Assumption**, reached via Church Street, sits on a small hill next to the manse. One of the island's best hotels occupies the remains of 18th-century Fort Young, once the town's main defence. Cruise passengers arriving at the Bayfront terminal in Roseau will find it a handy starting point for expeditions up into the Roseau Valley and to Morne Trois Pitons National Park in the central highlands.

Botanical Gardens

Within walking distance of the waterfront, this 16ha (40 acre) site nestles in the lee of Morne (Mount) Bruce on the edge of town. The gardens were established in 1890 on the site of a former sugar plantation. Today, the spreading lawns are a popular recreation area, with more than 150 different plants and trees, including a giant baobab tree (Dominica's national tree) pinning a school bus to

the ground exactly where it fell during Hurricane David in 1979.
East of the town centre. Open: daily 6am–dusk. Free admission.

Trafalgar Falls

A popular side-trip from the capital, minibuses trundle to within a ten-minute walk of these beautiful 61m (200ft) falls. From the car park, there is a short clamber up to the observation point – sensible shoes are a must. The twin falls cascade down either side of a towering green-cloaked cliff face, bounce on the riverbed boulders and cool the air with their spray. Guides lead expeditions up to a second vantage point, or down to the river, which is strewn with black and orange rocks – dyed by traces of iron in the water.
Roseau Valley (east of town). Free admission; charge for guides.

Carib Territory

This 1,500ha (3,700-acre) territory on the Atlantic coast of the island was given to descendants of the Carib people in 1903. Around 3,000 Caribs live here, though most are mixed-race these days, and have abandoned their simple thatched huts (carbets) in favour of wooden houses. You can get some excellent insight into Carib life at **Kalinago Barana Autê**, a recreated Carib village of thatch-roofed dwellings. Guides explain Carib ways of life, from the dugout canoes used for fishing to the woven baskets used to prepare cassava, a staple food. Traditional woven mats, hats, baskets and bags are on sale at the souvenir shops.
25km (16½ miles) northeast of Roseau. Kalinago Barana Autê. Old Coast Road, Crayfish River, Carib Territory. Tel: (767) 445 7979. Open: 10am–5pm mid-Oct to mid-April, closed Mon, mid-April to mid-Oct, closed Wed & Thur. Admission charge.

Morne Trois Pitons National Park

Designated a UNESCO World Heritage Site, this 6,880ha (17,000-acre) national park encompasses a great tract of primordial rainforest, mountains, lakes and sulphur springs. To reach many of the sights, such as the seething, volcanic **Boiling Lake**, and sulphurous fumaroles (volcanic vents) of the **Valley of Desolation**, a serious full-day hike is required.

However, the road into the park from Laudat gives access to the **Freshwater Lake** (at 762m/2,500ft above sea-level), and it is a pleasant two-hour return walk up to beautiful **Boeri Lake**. Alternatively, you could make tracks for the spectacular **Middleham Falls**. Island tours usually take in **Emerald Pool** on the east side of the park. A ten-minute walk from the roadside through the forest ends up at a pretty water grotto which is topped up by a tiny waterfall with a deep pool for swimming. You can also see the park from a **Rainforest Tram**, which traverses the canopy from Laudat.
10km (6 miles) northeast of Roseau. National Park Information.

Tel: (767) 448 2201.
Rainforest Trams.
Tel: (767) 440 3627; www.rfat.com.
Admission charge.

Portsmouth and the Northwest

Although Portsmouth is Dominica's second largest town, it's dusty, sleepy and, with the exception of a couple of hopeful T-shirt sellers, apparently quite unaffected by the activity of the small, modern but little-used Cabrits Cruise-Ship berth nearby. The town overlooks the thin black sand beaches and clear blue waters of wide, sheltered Prince Rupert Bay. Drake and Hawkins would stop off here to trade with the Caribs and resupply their ships, and the site was chosen for Dominica's first capital, later moved to Roseau.

Passengers disembarking here will find themselves immediately in the Cabrits National Park, where tour buses and taxi drivers are available.

The park is the only attraction in the immediate vicinity, though there is a picturesque cluster of brightly-painted rowboats for hire at the mouth of Indian River to the south of town, which take you along the river, used as a location in the *Pirates of the Caribbean* movies.

Cabrits National Park

On the north shore of Prince Rupert Bay, this national park incorporates the scattered remnants of Fort Shirley and assorted military outposts dating from 1765. The ruins of the 18th-century fort afford tremendous views across the bay, and there are various partially restored stone buildings dotted about the hillside lawns. Marked trails scramble up slippery, thickly wooded slopes to the crumbling Commandant's Quarters and other buildings swallowed up by the forest.
2km (1¼ miles) northwest of Portsmouth. Open: daily 9am–5pm. Admission charge.

Fisherman at Scotts Head village on Dominica's southwest coast

Grenada and Carriacou

Just 34km by 19km (21 by 12 miles), Grenada packs an astonishing variety of natural beauties into such a relatively small area. It is ringed by superb white sand beaches, while the mountainous interior climbs steeply past spice plantations, rainforests, gentle streams and cascading waterfalls to the island's highest point of Mt St Catherine (838m/2,757ft).

The 'Spice Isle of the Caribbean' lies at the southernmost tip of the Grenadines and is one of the world's chief producers of nutmeg, plus large quantities of mace (a by-product of the nutmeg tree), cloves, cinnamon and ginger. Here, you can literally smell spices on the breeze.

Columbus sighted the island on his third voyage in 1498. He named it Concepción, but future generations of Spanish sailors likened it to the hills of their native Granada, and the name stuck, albeit with a change of accent (it's pronounced Gre-nay-da) after a century of French occupation from 1650 onwards.

After years of fighting, the British finally gained control of Grenada in 1783, and kept it until independence in 1974. In 1979, following a bloodless coup, leftist Maurice Bishop seized power, aligning Grenada with Communist Cuba and the Soviet Union – much to the mortification of the US. The island became a pawn of the Cold War, and hit the world headlines in 1983, when US forces invaded to oust Bishop, who was placed under house arrest. Following public demonstrations in his support, he was freed, but was subsequently assassinated, some say by members of the army. Since then, things have returned to normal.

The island's tourist industry is one of the most carefully regulated in the region, with strict rules designed to preserve the environment: no building can stand taller than a palm tree, or be constructed less than 50m (165ft) back from the high-water mark. However, both the industry and the island suffered a devastating blow when Hurricane Ivan made a direct hit in September 2004. The 200kph (125mph) winds did terrible damage to both infrastructure and nature, but thankfully only the odd unreplaced roof or windblown tree remain as evidence of Ivan's impact.

Grenada Tourism Department

PO Box 293, The Carenage, St George's.
Tel: (473) 440 2279;
www.grenadagrenadines.com

Arrival

Ships dock at the spanking new
purpose-built Melville Street Cruise
Terminal in St George's; you exit
through the Esplanade Shopping Mall
and emerge just opposite the main
produce market on the Esplanade.
From here, you can explore the capital
on foot; turn right to reach the Sendall
Tunnel and the Carenage. Ships still
anchor in the Carenage if the Melville
Dock is full; tenders take passengers
directly to the Carenage waterfront.
Taxis await each ship just outside the
terminal and on the Carenage, and the
fixed fares to various destinations are
posted in the Welcome Centre within
the terminal. The bus station is just to
the left of the terminal, with minibuses
heading all over the island, and you can
also take water taxis from the Carenage
or Welcome Centre to Grand Anse
beach and other nearby spots.

St George's

Long-regarded as the prettiest harbour
in the Caribbean, St George's is backed
by a tight circle of hills formed by an
extinct volcanic crater. The mouth of
the harbour is guarded by the French-
built Fort George. Behind the
warehouses of the horseshoe-shaped
Carenage (inner harbour), pastel-
painted buildings cling to the

hillside lining the precipitous streets
like limpets.

The centre of St George's is located
west of the harbour across the hill.
If you visit on a Saturday, don't miss the
brilliant spice and produce market on
Market Square – it's one of the most
colourful and photogenic in the

Grenada and Carriacou

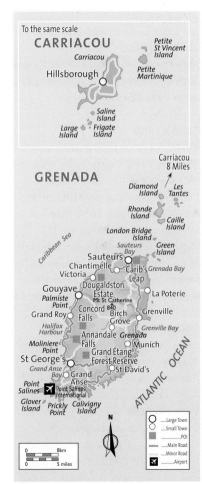

To the same scale

CARRIACOU

Petite
St Vincent
Island

Carriacou

Petite
Martinique

Hillsborough

Saline
Island

Large
Island

Frigate
Island

GRENADA

Carriacou
8 Miles

Diamond
Island

Les
Tantes

Rhonde
Island

Caille
Island

London Bridge
Island

Caribbean Sea

Sauteurs
Bay

Green
Island

Sauteurs

Chantimelle

Carib's

Grenada Bay

Victoria

Leap

Gouyave

Dougaldston
Estate

La Poterie

Palmiste
Point

Mt St Catherine

Concord

840

Grand Roy

Birch

Falls

Grove

Grenville

Halifax
Harbour

Grenville Bay

Moliniere
Point

Annandale
Falls

Grenada

Munich

Grand Étang

St George's

Forest Reserve

Grand Anse

St David's

Point

Grand

Salines

Anse

Glover

Point Salines
International

Caribbean Sea

Prickly
Point

Calivigny
Island

ATLANTIC OCEAN

N

0   8km

0   5 miles

○ ......Large Town
○ ......Small Town
■ ......POI
— ......Main Road
— ......Minor Road
✈ ......Airport

Caribbean. There's a helpful tourist office right on the pier with a supply of free maps to the island.

Grenada National Museum

This small museum is housed in the old French army barracks (built 1704), on the west side of the Carenage. It covers local history and culture from the earliest Caribs to the present day, including ancient artefacts, colonial knick-knacks and a look at events leading up to the invasion of 1983.

Monckton St, off Young St. Tel: (473) 440 3725. Open: Mon–Fri 9am–4.30pm, Sat 10am–1pm. Admission charge.

Carib's Leap

The 30.5m (100ft) high Carib's Leap cliff rears straight up from the sea. In 1651 the last of the island's Carib Indians preferred to jump off here and thus commit suicide rather than surrender to French colonists. This tragic event is also recalled in the name of the nearby settlement of Sauteurs (in French, 'the leapers'). Just above the cliff, there's a small museum dedicated to the Caribs, including a model of a typical village.

32km (20 miles) northeast of St George's. Museum. Open: 10am–5pm daily. Admission charge.

Concord Falls

There are three waterfalls here in the Concord Valley. The lowest is accessible from the coast road and is a popular spot on any tour of the island. You can

---

CARRIACOU

An occasional stop for smaller cruise ships, the diminutive island of Carriacou (13km by 8km/8 by 5 miles) is famed for its smuggling, its schooners, and the locals' tolerance for Jack Iron rum, a spirit so eye-swivellingly strong (160 per cent proof) that it causes ice to sink.

Hillsborough is the main settlement, with a bustling waterfront where you can see the graceful cedar schooners, locally built, and a Historical Museum in a restored cotton ginnery (mill) on Paterson Street. The beaches are gorgeous, but don't overdo the Jack Iron or you may miss your boat!

---

swim in the natural pool for a nominal fee. It is a 25-minute hike up to the second fall, and another hour-plus to the 20m (65ft) tall top fall.

11km (7 miles) northeast of St George's.

Dougaldston Estate

Most of the island's spices are grown on this 324ha (800 acre) spice plantation, and although it has fallen on hard times, it still makes a fascinating visit. Inside the old wooden 'factory', you'll get an introduction to a wide variety of spices from cinnamon and cloves to tonka beans (a vanilla substitute) and allspice. All the while, a local guide explains the old-style processing methods (it's customary to tip the guide). Mixed bags of spices only cost a couple of dollars, and make a great potpourri.

14km (8½ miles) north of St George's. Open: Mon–Fri 9am–4pm, Sat 10am–1pm. Free admission.

Gouyave

Though 'Gouyave' comes from the French word for 'guava', this little clapboard town is the nutmeg capital of Grenada. Nutmeg was introduced to the island from the East Indies by British planters in the 1830s. As one of the world's top producers, Grenada even features the nutmeg on its national flag. Take a tour around the **Grenada Nutmeg Cooperative** for the low-down on this spice and its waxy byproduct, mace.

14.5km (9 miles) north of St George's.
Grenada Nutmeg Cooperative.
Open: Mon–Fri 8am–4pm.
Admission charge.

Grande Anse Bay

This is the best beach on the island for day trippers. It comprises 3km (2 miles) of gleaming white sands, with watersports, shopping and dining facilities.

5km (3 miles) south of St George's.

Grand Étang and Annandale Falls

High in the Central Mountain Range, the 12ha (30-acre) Grand Étang crater lake nestles in the forest, a cool 530m (1,740ft) above sea level. There are forest trails and walks around the lake – it takes about an hour to go all the way around. Keep an eye out for the mona monkeys introduced from West Africa more than 350 years ago.

Closer to St George's, the Annandale Falls and its visitor centre is another favourite stop along the road. The 9m (30ft) high waterfall splashes down into a bathing pool, bordered by a herb and spice garden. Park guides give narrated walks, and there are refreshments, crafts and spice stalls, and swimming too.

11km (7 miles) north of St George's.
Grand Étang Forest Reserve and Visitor Centre. Tel: (473) 440 2452.
Open: daily 8am–4pm & Sun when cruise ships are in. Admission charge.
Annandale Falls Visitor Centre. Open: daily 8am–5pm.

Brightly painted boats drawn up on the sands of Grand Anse Bay

Pirates of the Caribbean

The dastardly likes of Henry Morgan, Edward Teach (Blackbeard), 'Calico' Jack Rackham (so-called for his predilection for striped pants) and their cut-throat, rum-swigging, peg-legged cronies really did exist – and they caused havoc around the Caribbean region during the 16th and 17th centuries.

The region's early 'sailors of fortune' were known as *boucaniers* or buccaneers, a name derived from French hunter-adventurers who made a living from supplying passing ships with dried meat, cured in smokehouses called *boucanes*. Ambitious buccaneers soon abandoned the victualling trade to pursue richer pickings in the form of Spanish galleons. Laden with gold and precious gems from the New World, these floating treasure houses made tempting targets, and many buccaneers made the transition to a life of piracy via a spell as an officially sanctioned privateer. Armed with a government licence, or Letter of Marque, privateers were authorised to capture enemy ships in times of war. Once hostilities ceased, however, few felt inclined to resume a law-abiding lifestyle, and the buccaneer-privateers (also called freebooters or filibusters) soon turned buccaneer-pirates.

An exception was Henry Morgan, a notorious pirate-turned-privateer, who was appointed to rally the notorious Jamaican buccaneers during England's war with Spain in 1668. Morgan went on to capture and destroy the Spanish South American capital at Panama, then retired to his handsome estates

Though many have searched for buccaneer gold, little has been found

in Jamaica, where he was elected Deputy Governor, and became the scourge of his former comrades.

True pirates of the Caribbean owed allegiance to no one, however. They terrorised shipping from the Caribbean to North Carolina, occasional home of Edward Teach, better known as Blackbeard. Famed for roaring into battle with half a dozen pistols (three in each hand), and the pigtails of his beard spliced with lighted fuses, he was a frequent visitor to Port Royal, Jamaica, described in a London newspaper of the 1690s as the 'dunghill of the universe'. Other pirate hotspots included the Virgin Islands, and the tricky seas and secluded cays of the Bahama Islands.

But the golden age of Caribbean piracy was nearing its end. Governor Woodes Rogers arrived to clear up the Bahamas in 1718, the same year the Royal Navy caught up with Blackbeard. Defiant to the last, it is said Teach's decapitated body swam several laps around the ship before it sank. Calico Jack was surprised during a drunken revel in Jamaica, tried, hanged and left to rot on Rackham's Cay, off Kingston, in 1720. During the trial, two of his shipmates were discovered to be women, Anne Bonney and Mary Read, as ruthless a pair of bloodthirsty pirates as ever there was.

Tales of buried treasure and dastardly pirates abound in Caribbean folklore

Although tales of hidden pirate treasure abound, little has ever been found. Several sunken, treasure-laden Spanish galleons have been discovered, but most were victims of hurricanes and hidden reefs, not pirates. The most famous of the sunken galleons is the *Nuestra Señora de Atocha* found by Mel Fisher off the Florida Keys. Dive expeditions to the Atocha are available.

Guadeloupe and St Barthélemy (St Barts)

Shaped like a butterfly with two mismatched wings, the French-owned island of Guadeloupe is an unusual place. The western 'wing', Basse-Terre, is mountainous, rain-forested and dominated by the steaming Soufrière volcano. Grande-Terre, the northeastern 'wing', is flat, dry and more developed, with its white-sand beaches proving a magnet for visitors.

GUADELOUPE

Sighted by Columbus in 1493, Guadeloupe was deemed one of the 'Cannibal Isles', and subsequently given a wide berth until 1635, when French settlers arrived to drive out the remaining Caribs. In terms of French priorities, the island played second fiddle to Martinique for years, though there was a brief moment of glory in 1794, when Guadeloupean patriots overthrew the planters and installed a revolutionary government under Victor Hugues. (Martinique's planters and businessmen steadfastly maintained the pre-Revolutionary status quo.)

Guadeloupean slaves were freed, and Hugues erected the mandatory guillotine on the main square in Pointe-à-Pitre, where 300 enemies of the Revolution lost their heads. When Paris reintroduced slavery from 1802 until 1848, many freed Guadeloupean slaves preferred death to submission. Today, Guadeloupe remains an overseas department of France, with a decidedly Gallic feel – you'll pay for your wine, cheese, baguettes and café au lait in euros.

Arrival

Ships dock at the Centre St-John Perse terminal in the heart of downtown Pointe-à-Pitre on Grand-Terre. From here, you're within walking distance of the town's attractions and the tourist office (follow the quayside to Place de la Victoire). Ships are welcomed by English-speaking hostesses who can point you in the direction of an English-speaking taxi driver. Taxis are metred and rates are set by the government with typical fares posted at the stand outside the port.

Guadeloupe Office Départemental du Tourisme

5 square de la Banque, 97163 Pointe-à-Pitre. Tel: (590) 82 09 30; www.lesilesdeguadeloupe.com

A rainforest path near the Maison de la Forêt in the Parc Naturel de Guadeloupe

Grande-Terre

The main attractions on low-lying Grande-Terre are its beaches, and the best of these are found on the south coast between Gosier and St François. Gosier is the most touristy of the three seaside towns along this stretch. Both Ste Anne and St François are former fishing ports, though most of the fishing these days is done by tourists who enjoy the excellent sport fishing.

Fort Fleur d'Epée

Midway between Pointe-à-Pitre and Gosier and shaded by flaming Flamboyant (royal poinciana) trees, the ruins of these 18th-century coral rock fortifications afford fine views across the bay to Gosier, down the Basse-Terre coast to Pointe Capesterre, and across to the islands of Marie-Galante and La Désirade.

Place St-François in the quiet Guadeloupe capital of Basse-Terre

Open: Mon 10am–5pm, Tue–Sun 9am–5pm. Tel: (590) 90 94 61. Free admission.

Pointe-à-Pitre

Guadeloupe's main cruise-ship port and largest town, Pointe-à-Pitre is an unattractive port with congested streets and frenetic waterfront markets. However, you can relax in the cafés around place de la Victoire, the central gardens shaded by palm, mango and African tulip trees, cooled by fountains and edged by a clutch of venerable Colonial-style buildings.

Nearby, there is a small flower market outside the **Cathedral of St Peter and St Paul**, with its iron frame bolted together like an elaborate Meccano set. Close to here, off rue Frébault, is the marvellous **Covered Market**, piled high with spices and sunhats, and staffed by garrulous stallholders.

A short walk away on rue Peynier, a pretty pink French townhouse with wrought-iron decorations and a double staircase houses the **Musée Schoelcher** (*Open: Mon–Fri 9am–5pm. Admission charge*). Here, you will find assorted mementoes of the famous French abolitionist who led the fight against slavery in the 19th century, together with collections of African ivories, model ships, ceramics and other curios. A few blocks to the east on the corner of rue Noizières and rue Achille René-Boisneuf, the exhibits at **Musée St-Jean Perse** (*Open: Mon–Fri 9am–5pm, Sat 9am–noon. Admission charge*) are centred on the life of Guadeloupean poet Saint-Jean Perse, who won the Nobel Prize for Literature in 1960.

Basse-Terre

The administrative capital of Guadeloupe is a small, sleepy town tucked in the lee of the central highlands, about an hour's drive from Pointe-à-Pitre. Founded in 1643, Basse-Terre has several fine public buildings, a cathedral dating back to the 17th century, and the rambling ramparts of **Fort St Charles** (also known as Fort Delgrés), on the southern edge of town. Founded in 1650 and enlarged over the centuries, the fort now houses a small local history museum.

Museum. Open: daily 8am–4.30pm. Free admission.

Ilets Pigeon

Frequent glass-bottomed boat tours depart for short trips out to this tiny island reserve just off the west coast. The underwater panorama is also known as the Cousteau Reserve, after the famous diver, Jacques Cousteau, declared it to be one of the best dive sites he'd ever seen. It's still spectacular, with visibility up to 24m (80ft), revealing superb corals and dazzling marine life.

Offshore of Plage Malendure.

Jardin Botanique de Deshaies

Just outside the village of Deshaies, this beautifully laid out garden contains a host of tropical flowers, plants and trees, as well as loriquets and parrots.

Deshaies. Open: daily 9.30am–4.30pm. Admission charge.

Maison du Bois

Local woodcrafts are on show at this museum in the cabinet-making centre of Pointe Noire. Sections devoted to tools and domestic utensils from the pre-electric era include wicker lobster pots and hand whisks, plus machines for seeding cotton, grinding coffee and for building wheels and boats. There is a furniture showroom and a mini arboretum in the grounds.

Pointe Noire. Open: Tue–Sun 9.30am–5pm. Admission charge.

Musée du Rhum (Museum of Rum)

An exhaustive and detailed history of rum (with English translations) is enlivened by some evocative early 20th-century photographs of local merchants and craftspeople. These candid shots of the laundress and the sorbet maker, the milk ladies and the fish trap workers are reason enough to visit, but rum-lovers will also be offered an opportunity to sample the product after viewing a short film and taking a look at the various exhibits. A juice vat hewn out of a single tree trunk is particularly impressive.

Open: Mon–Sat 9am–5pm. Admission charge.

Parc Naturel de Guadeloupe

Covering some 30,000 hectares (74,000 acres) of corrugated slopes smothered with lush rainforest, and encompassing the La Soufrière volcano, Basse-Terre's fantastic national park is a designated UNESCO biosphere reserve. The park is networked by 300km (185 miles) of well-marked hiking trails making some of its most beautiful parts accessible on foot; you can also drive right through the park via the Route de la Traversée. This cross-island road between Grand-Terre and Basse-Terre skims westwards past sugar-cane fields lined with African tulip trees (stunning in July), before climbing up into the Parc National and crossing the Col des Mamelles. This pass affords stunning views of the aptly named twin volcanic peaks of Les Mamelles ('The Breasts'). The **Maison de la Forêt park information centre** (*Open: Wed–Mon 9am–1.15pm & 2–4.30pm. Closed: Tue*) on the Route de la Traversée has trail maps and brochures on the local flora and fauna, and is the start of several trails.

Cascade aux Écrevisses Just inside the Parc Naturel and off the Route de la Traversée, this waterfall gushes from the hillside near the road. Sure-footed explorers can scramble around the boulders at this favourite picnic spot.

Chûtes du Carbet Fed by the Grand Carbet River, which originates in La Soufrière, these popular waterfalls come in three tiers. The 110m (360ft) high second spill is the most easily visited, just a 20-minute walk through the rainforest.
Northwest of St Sauveur.

La Soufrière
The highest point in the Eastern Caribbean at 1,467m (4,318ft) above sea level, the sulphurous Soufrière crater is an eerie, nightmarish landscape of bubbling mud pools, bizarre lava formations and wisps of steam. Eruptions and major earth movements were noted in 1695, 1797, 1837, 1956 and 1976. Vehicles can venture as far as the Savane à Mulets, 305m (1,000ft) short of the crater, from where marked footpaths lead up the volcano. The steep hike takes around two hours, but note that you are officially not allowed right to the top for safety reasons.

Maison du Volcan Perched on the forested slopes of La Soufrière above Basse-Terre, the Maison du Volcan acts as an unofficial visitor centre for the volcano, providing a potted introduction to vulcanism and the region's origins. The setting on the hill is lovely; there is an appreciable drop in temperature, and you can see a fair number of old Creole-style planters' houses nestled against the hillside.
St-Claude. Open: daily 10am–6pm. Free admission.

ST BARTHÉLEMY
More commonly known as St Barts, this pint-sized (23sq km/9sq mile) volcanic dot lies 200km (125 miles) northwest of Guadeloupe. It's quite simply the most chic spot in the Caribbean, with exquisite beaches, exclusive shopping and gourmet restaurants which will delight style-conscious Francophiles but not those on a budget.

First settled by French sailors from Brittany and Normandy, St Barts spent 100 years under Swedish rule during the 18th and 19th centuries, hence the name of the capital, Gustavia. Catch up on the island's history here at the **Musée de St Barthélemy** on the west side of the harbour (*Open: Mon 2.30–6pm, Tue–Fri 8.30am–12.30pm & 2–6pm, Sat 9am–noon. Admission charge*). And, don't miss the delightful fishing village of **Corossol**, just north of Gustavia, a picture-book Breton community dropped into a tropical setting; some older ladies still wear traditional, frilly, starched Breton sun bonnets. The best beaches are on the south coast at Anse du Gouverneur (no facilities) and Anse de Grande Saline; Anse des Flamands, in the north, has a couple of hotels.

Arrival

Cruise ships anchor in Gustavia Harbour, and passengers are brought ashore by tender. From the quay, you can easily explore the town on foot. Although the island is tiny, you won't want to walk further than the town itself; taxis line up along the harbour, and fares are set (but not cheap).

St Barts Office Municipal du Tourisme
quai Général de Gaulle, 97133 Gustavia. Tel: (590) 27 87 27; www.st-barths.com

Guadeloupe and St Barthélemy

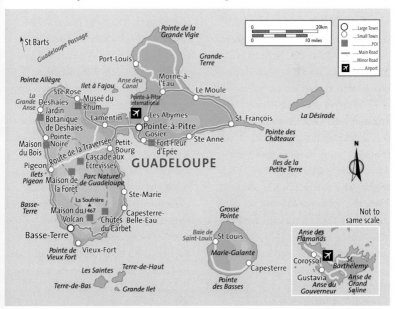

Jamaica

More than 1,100km (700 miles) south of Miami, Jamaica is the third largest of the Caribbean islands (11,424sq km/ 4,411sq miles), and a natural beauty with jungle-clad mountains, rushing rivers and superb beaches. Christopher Columbus reckoned it to be 'the fairest island that eyes have beheld'. Noël Coward, Errol Flynn, Ian Fleming (author of the James Bond novels) and a host of other famous devotees have lived here or found themselves returning time and time again, captivated by the island's physical beauty and the easy-going charm of its people.

When Columbus first landed here in 1494, the island was called Xaymaca ('Land of Wood and Water') by the peaceable Arawak Indians who inhabited it. The first permanent Spanish settlement was founded on the north coast in 1510, and the Arawaks were forced into slavery. Within a century, the estimated native population of around 100,000 had been wiped out. Many fell victim to European diseases; others were hunted for sport.

The English captured Jamaica from Spain in 1655, and set about turning the island into the world's largest sugar producer, using thousands of West African slaves who were bought and sold at slave markets in Kingston and along the north coast. From the latter part of the 17th century up until the abolition of slavery in 1834, the colonists flourished. And more than a few of them (such as Henry Morgan), made the switch to the 'respectable' and luxurious planter's lifestyle after

earning their fortunes on the high seas as buccaneers. Some slaves managed to escape and hide in the inaccessible mountain territory of Cockpit Country in the central west highlands. Known as Maroons, they waged a sporadic guerrilla war against the planters and government. The most famous slave revolt was led by Sam Sharpe in 1831, today one of Jamaica's national heroes. Finally, in 1834, the Emancipation Act gave freedom to all slaves, though this only became reality after a subsequent four-year tied 'apprenticeship' period to the plantation. Former slaves claimed what land they could and turned to agriculture with the help of Christian missionaries. A century of political experimentation and the growing 1930s nationalist movement led to the creation of trade unions, political parties, and a new constitution in 1944; by 1962, Jamaica had become the first British colony in the Caribbean to achieve independence.

Jamaica

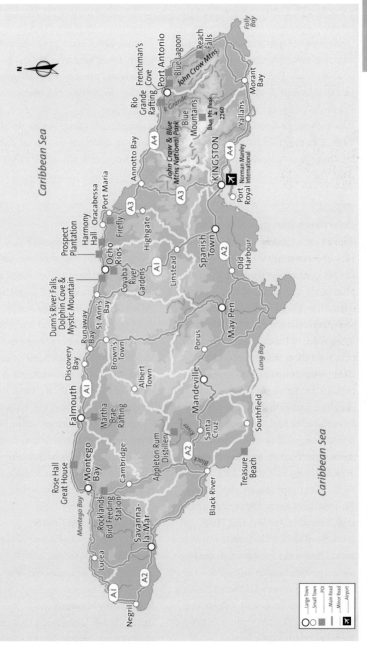

Caribbean Sea

N

Folly
Bay

Reach
Falls

Port Antonio
Blue Lagoon
Frenchman's
Cove
John Crow Mtns
Rio
Grande Rafting
R Grande
Blue
Mountains
Blue Mt Peak
2260
Morant
Bay

Yallahs

A4

John Crow & Blue
Mtns National Park

Annotto Bay

A3

KINGSTON

A3

A4

Port Norman Manley
Royal International

Port Maria
Oracabessa
Harmony
Hall
Firefly

Prospect
Plantation

Ocho
Rios

Highgate

A1

Linstead

Spanish
Town

A2

Old
Harbour

Coyaba
River
Gardens

Dunn's River Falls,
Dolphin Cove &
Mystic Mountain

Runaway
Bay St Ann's
Bay

Brown's
Town

Porus

May Pen

Discovery
Bay

A1

Albert
Town

Mandeville

Long Bay

Falmouth

Martha
Brae
Rafting

Southfield

Appleton Rum
Distillery

Santa
Cruz

Black River

Treasure
Beach

Montego
Bay

Cambridge

A2

Rose Hall
Great House

Rocklands
Bird Feeding
Station

Montego Bay

Savanna-
la-Mar

Lucea

A2

A1

Negril

Caribbean Sea

0   12km
0   8 miles

Large Town
Small Town
POI
Main Road
Minor Road
Airport

Jamaica's two main cruise ports are on the north coast, at Montego Bay and Ocho Rios, though some smaller cruise lines also use Port Antonio further east.

Jamaica Tourist Board

PO Box 67, Gloucester Ave, Cornwall Beach, Montego Bay. Tel: (876) 952 4425. There are also information booths at the cruise ship ports (see also *www.visitjamaica.com*).

Arrival

Ocho Rios is Jamaica's cruising capital, with a host of nearby attractions that entice two or more ships per day into her port during the winter high season. Ships dock at the Port of Ocho Rios, adjacent to the Island Village shopping and entertainment complex, which has its own slip of beach. The main town beach is a short walk from the terminal (turn left as you exit), and you can also explore the downtown area, with its duty-free malls and craft market, on foot. However to get to the town's other attractions, you'll need a taxi. Cars line up outside the dock awaiting passengers.

In Montego Bay, ships dock at the Cruise Ship Terminal on the Freeport Peninsula, a fifteen-minute drive from the Gloucester Avenue 'Hip Strip', location of the beaches, restaurants and bars. There are a few stores in the open-air shopping complex adjacent to the complex, but otherwise there's nothing to see on foot. Taxis wait outside the terminal and can ferry you into town or to sights around the island.

The few ships that dock at Port Antonio tie up at the Errol Flynn Marina, which has a pool and a slip of beach, From here, you can easily explore the town on foot. Drivers wait outside the marina exit when there's a ship in port.

Jamaican taxis are not metered, so agree on a fare before you set out. Minibuses serve almost all of the island, but aren't really recommended for the casual visitor.

Kingston

The island's capital since 1872, Kingston sprang up after the infamous buccaneering base of Port Royal slid into the sea as a result of an earthquake in 1692. Today, this is the seat of government and business and boasts a population of more than one million.

Kingston lacks charm but offers a handful of cultural attractions. A favourite escape from the downtown maelstrom is the short drive along the Palisadoes to the former site of Port Royal, where the ramparts of Fort Charles afford views back to the Blue Mountains, and there is a small maritime and history museum.

Kingston Tourism Centre

PO Box 360, 2 St Lucia Ave, Kingston. Tel: (876) 929 9200.
Also see: www.jamaicatravel.com

Bob Marley Museum

Reggae music fans should visit this memorial to Trench Town's most

famous son, set in his former home, with hordes of artefacts, from guitars to gold discs, and a couple of rooms left as they were when he lived here.
56 Hope Rd. Tel: (876) 927 9152; www.bobmarley-foundation.com/museum.html. Open: Mon–Fri 9.30am–5pm. Admission charge.

Devon House
A restored 19th-century great house with souvenir shops and restaurants in the former stables. The interior boasts fine antique furnishings.
26 Hope Rd. Tel: (876) 929 6602. www.devonhousejamaica.com. Open: Mon–Sat 9.30am–5pm. Admission charge for the house.

Hope Botanical Gardens
Established in 1881, these 81ha (200-acre) botanical gardens provide an explosion of marvellous colour, shady paths, sweeping lawns, and elegant royal palms. There's also a vegetarian restaurant and children's zoo to visit, though the latter has seen better days.
Old Hope Rd. Tel: (876) 927 1257. Gardens. Open: 6am–6pm. Zoo. Open: 10am–5pm. Admission charge to zoo; free admission to park.

National Gallery of Art
This is one of the best permanent displays of Caribbean art in the region, rich in oil paintings, drawings, sculpture and wood carvings. Notable names in the modern Jamaican art world include painters David Pottinger and Barrington

A mural representing Bob Marley, Kingston

Watson, and sculptors Christopher González and Edna Manley.
Orange St (at Ocean Blvd). Tel: (876) 922 1561. www.galleryjamaica.com. Open: Tue–Thur 10am–4.30pm, Fri 10am–4pm, Sat 10am–3pm. Admission charge.

THE BLUE MOUNTAINS
Crowded into the eastern corner of the island, the spectacular Blue Mountains soar up to Blue Mountain Peak, which tops 2,254m (7,402ft). The climb begins the minute you leave Kingston, with the two roads through the range heading north to the former military base at Newcastle and on to the Holywell Recreational Park, usually swathed in mist; halfway up, stop off at the wonderful Strawberry Hill hotel for a drink or a bite to eat with spectacular views over the capital. The other road leads northeast to Mavis Bank; you can see the region's prized Blue Mountain coffee being processed at the JABLUM factory and purchase a hoard of the aromatic beans to take home.

Spanish Town

The original capital of Jamaica for more than 300 years, Spanish Town lies 22.5km (14 miles) west of Kingston. Though founded by the Spanish in 1523, the colonial-style Georgian stone buildings lend a distinctly British air to the town centre, where British naval hero, Admiral Rodney (inexplicably attired in Roman garb), strikes a commanding pose over the main square, known as The Park. On The Park a former governor's residence, the **King's House**, is home to a museum of folk crafts and colonial period furnishings, while 5km (3 miles) east on the road to Kingston, the **White Marl Arawak Museum** pays tribute to Jamaica's earliest inhabitants.
King's House. Open: Mon–Thur 9.30am–4.30pm, Fri 9.30am–3.30pm. Free admission.
White Marl Arawak Museum. Open: Mon–Fri 9am–4pm. Admission charge.

Montego Bay

'Mo' Bay' is Jamaica's second largest town, but number one in the island's tourism stakes. 'Montego' is derived from the Spanish manteca, meaning 'pig fat', from the days when sailors would come ashore here to hunt wild hogs. At the start of the 20th century it became fashionable to bathe at Doctor's Cave Beach, and the rest, as they say, is history. A pristine strip of white sand lapped by turquoise waters, with changing facilities and places to eat and drink, Doctor's Cave is the centrepiece of Gloucester Avenue, also known as the 'Hip Strip', lined with tourist-oriented restaurants and bars and with a couple of other nice beaches, too.
Doctor's Cave Beach. Open: daily 8.30am–sunset. Tel: (876) 952 2566; www.doctorscavebathingclub.com. Admission charge.

Appleton Rum Distillery

Up in the hills of Cockpit Country, the Appleton Estate produces Jamaica's most famous rum. After a tour of the distillery, there are tastings and the opportunity to buy some of the products at excellent prices.
Siloah, 30km (20 miles) southeast of Montego Bay. Tel: (876) 963 9215. www.appletonrumtour.com. Open: Mon–Fri 9am–3.30pm. Admission charge.

Rocklands Bird Feeding Station

Perched in the hills above the settlement of Anchovy, this is a great chance to get close to Jamaica's diverse and beautiful bird life. Hundreds of darting, chattering birds gather for the afternoon feeding sessions first initiated by the late Lisa Salmon in 1958. Many of the diners are tame enough to feed from your hand.
9.5km (6 miles) south of Montego Bay. Tel: (876) 952 2009. Open: daily 2–5pm. Admission charge.

Rose Hall Great House

The most famous house in Jamaica – possibly the whole Caribbean – largely

Doctor's Cave Beach was a fashionable health resort in the early 1900s

by virtue of its legendary mistress, Annie Palmer, who was also known as the 'White Witch of Rose Hall'. The 19th-century femme fatale is credited with bumping off three husbands and numerous slave lovers before being murdered in her bed. Guides in period dress lay it on thick as you tour the restored interior.

13km (8 miles) northeast of Montego Bay. Tel: (876) 953 2323. Open: daily 9am–6pm. Admission charge.

Port Antonio

Founded in 1723, this is the resort that time forgot – almost. Built on a point dividing two stunning bays, with the Blue Mountains in the background, Port Antonio's setting is truly fabulous. A booming banana boat port and resort at the beginning of the 20th century, the town's fortunes took a dive. Though the screen idol Errol Flynn bought Navy Island just offshore, and turned it into a Hollywood hideaway for his fellow stars in the 1940s and 1950s, Port Antonio has never fully

recovered top resort status. Many of the buildings along the main street are worse for wear but the waterfront has been spruced up by the construction of the **Errol Flynn Marina**, complete with oceanside promenades and a good restaurant.

The local sights are pretty low-key, starting with the stunning **Blue Hole** (better known as Hollywood's Blue Lagoon), and the picture-perfect beach at Frenchman's Cove.

Ocho Rios and excursions

Midway along the north coast, 105km (65 miles) east of Montego Bay, the former fishing village of Ocho Rios has been given the full mass tourism development treatment and emerged as a seamless chain of hotels and burger franchises fringed by packed beaches. This is also Jamaica's busiest cruise ship destination. Duty-free shopping is within walking distance of the pier at the Island Village complex, but unless you want to spend the rest of the day on the beach, you will need transport to reach the local attractions.

Rose Hall, home of *femme fatale* Annie Palmer

Coyaba River Gardens and Museum

The name comes from the Arawak word for 'paradise' and the museum occupies the grounds of the old Shaw Park Hotel, in turn built on the site of an ancient Amerindian settlement. It traces Jamaica's history and cross-cultural influences from the Arawaks and Spanish, through the colonial period, right up to the present day. Take time to admire the gardens, investigate the gallery and relax over a cup of home-grown Blue Mountain coffee or climb the picturesque Mahoe Falls, overlooked by a wooden walkway that also affords a panoramic view over Ocho Rios.

Shaw Park Estate, 4km (2½ miles) south of Ocho Rios.
www.coyabagardens.com.
Open: daily 8am–5pm.
Admission charge.

Dunn's River Falls

Probably the single most popular outing for visitors to the island, these deliciously cool mountain falls tumble 183m (600ft) down to the sea over a series of easily climbable ledges. Check in your clothes and valuables at the ticket entrance lockers, and join the swimsuit-clad 'daisy chain' (a human conga line rallied by sure-footed guides) on the slippery route to the top. The ascent takes about 40 minutes.

Off the A1, 3km (2 miles) west of Ocho Rios.
Tel: (876) 974 2857.
Open: 8.30am–4pm, cruise ship days Wed–Fri 7am–4pm.
Admission charge.

Firefly

Playwright and professional wit Noël Coward purchased this magnificent

305m (1,000ft) high crow's nest site in the 1940s, and must have spent much of his last 23 years admiring the incredible views. In fact, it is such a good lookout that buccaneer Henry Morgan is reputed to have used the tumbledown limestone building below the house as a shore retreat.

The interior of Firefly has been left exactly as it was when Coward lived there, right down to his silk pyjamas hanging in the wardrobe, and there are paintings, photographs and other memorabilia on display. Coward is buried in the garden beneath a plain marble tomb and a statue of him sits overlooking the coastline.

Off the A3, 34km (21 miles) east of Ocho Rios. Tel: (876) 997 7201. Open: daily 8.30am–5.30pm. Admission charge.

Harmony Hall

This attractively restored late-18th-century country house, with its intricate gingerbread fretwork, makes an inviting gallery for the works of contemporary Jamaican artists. Visiting exhibitions are a feature, and souvenir hunters will find a good range of top-quality craft items. There is also a bar, restaurant and garden terrace.

Off the A3, 6.5km (4 miles) east of Ocho Rios. Tel: (876) 974 2870; www.harmonyhall.com. Open: daily 10am–6pm. Free admission.

Mystic Mountain

This new attraction offers several exhilarating options, from swinging through the treetops on the Tranopy zipline to floating through the forest canopy on an open Skylift Explorer gondola or taking an adrenaline-charged ride on the bobsleigh track from the pretty Railway Station, which affords gorgeous views down the coast. There's also an exhibition on Jamaican culture, and a lovely infinity pool if you fancy a dip. Just uphill from Dunn's River, a visit can also be combined with climbing the falls.

Dunn's River. Tel: (876) 974 3990; www.rainforestrams.com. Admission charge.

Prospect Plantation

The 405ha (1,000-acre) Prospect estate is one of Jamaica's finest working plantations, cultivating bananas, cassava, cocoa, pawpaws, pimentos and sugar cane among other crops. Entertaining, narrated tours aboard an old-fashioned jitney (canopied open wagon) take around an hour, and include dramatic views of the White River Gorge, a stop at Sir Harold's Viewpoint for a panoramic vista of the coast, and an avenue of trees planted by such famous visitors as Charlie Chaplin and Sir Winston Churchill. If you fancy a spot of horse- or even camel-riding, call in advance and they will have a suitable steed awaiting you on your arrival.

Off the A3, 5km (3 miles) east of Ocho Rios. Tel: (876) 994 13731058; www.prospectplantationtours.com. Open: daily for tours at 10.30am, 2pm & 3.30pm. Admission charge.

Martinique

Renowned for the beauty of its flora and its beaches, Martinique was spotted by Columbus on either his second or fourth trip, but not settled until 1635. Apart from a couple of brief foreign incursions during the 18th century, the island has remained indisputably Gallic, and is a fully fledged region of France. French is the first (and often only) language, and the euro is the local currency.

Martinique is one of the larger islands in the Lesser Antilles (measuring 100km by 37km/62 miles by 23 miles), so plan your time ashore with care. A visit to the mountainous green heart of the island, dominated by the ominous volcanic bulk of Mont Pelée and with some of the Caribbean's most spectacular rainforest, is a 'must', while the capital, Fort-de-France, is a shopper's delight. To the south, rippling cane fields stretch off to the horizon behind some of those famous beaches.

Martinique Office du Tourisme
Immeuble Le Beaupré, Pointe de Jahem. Tel: (596) 61 61 77; www.martinique.org. There's also an information booth at the Pointe Simon cruise ship terminal.

Arrival
Most ships dock at the Pointe Simon cruise ship terminal, right in the heart of Fort-de-France and within walking distance of its sights. If Pointe Simon is full, you might also dock at the passenger terminal in the main Maritime Harbour; tenders transport you to the terminal, from where you'll need a taxi to get into the capital. Taxis await ships at both ports, and all are metred. Most will offer a flat rate for a sightseeing tour, however.

Fort-de-France
Clambering up the steep hillsides behind the Baie des Flamands, the capital's narrow streets pack closely

JOSÉPHINE

An 18th-century Martiniquan fortune-teller once read the palms of two cousins on the island and foretold that one would become an empress, the other 'more than an empress'.

The former became Napoleon's Empress Joséphine. Her simple childhood home, **La Pagerie**, can be visited near Les Trois-Ilets (26km/16 miles south of Fort-de-France). The other was kidnapped by Barbary pirates and taken to Istanbul, where she became the Turkish sultan's favourite concubine, the Sultana Validé.

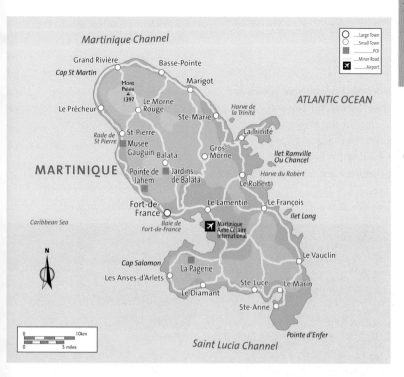

around the attractive 5ha (12-acre) **Jardin Savane** on the harbour. The statue of Emperor Napoleon's Empress Joséphine lost its head in 1995 when locals marking her role in reinstating slavery on the island removed it.

Behind rue de la Liberté, the main shopping district is bordered by rue Victor-Hugo and rue Victor-Sévère. The Cathedral of St-Louis is here too, on rue Schoelcher.

If the beach is your prime objective, there is a convenient ferry service from the Fort-de-France waterfront to four of the best beaches close to the capital. Plage Pointe du Bout offers a man-made strip of white sand lined with luxury hotels; Plage Anse-Mitan is also well-supplied with hotels and beach bars, and has good snorkelling; the narrow, sandy crescent of Plage Anse à l'Ane has plenty of shade and a couple of small hotel-restaurants; and Plage Grande-Anse is the most basic, with piles of fishermen's nets, laid-back beach bars and boats for hire.

Musée Départemental d'Archéologie et de Préhistoire (Archeology and Prehistory Museum)

This museum houses exhibits on slavery, colonial life and some notable pre-Columbian artefacts (*9 rue de la*

Liberté. Open: Mon 1–5pm, Tue–Fri 8am–5pm, Sat 9am–noon. Admission charge).

Nouvelle Bibliothèque Schoelcher (New Schoelcher Library)

Facing the top left-hand corner of the park, the runaway Byzantine-Egyptian-Art Nouvelle Bibliothèque Schoelcher was built for the 1889 Paris Exposition, and transported here piece by piece. It is named after Victor Schoelcher, a leading light in the 19th-century movement to abolish slavery in the French West Indies.

Tel: (596) 702 667. Open: Mon 1–5.30pm, Tue–Fri 8.30am–5.30pm, Sat 8.30am–noon. Free admission.

Balata

Sacré-Coeur de Balata

One glimpse at the Montmartre martiniquais, and you could be

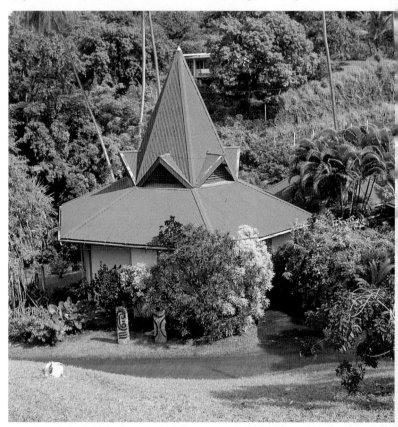

The Musée Gauguin at Anse Turin also displays work by local artists

forgiven for thinking you are hallucinating. This mini replica of the famous Parisian basilica was erected in 1923 as a memorial to the dead of World War I.
8km (5 miles) north of Fort-de-France.

Jardin de Balata

These glorious gardens are not to be missed. Massed hibiscus, poinsettias, bougainvillea and plumes of red ginger glow in the sunlight, while glossy anthurium and pink torch ginger thrive in the shade. All around are ferns, fruit trees, spice bushes and variegated immortelles. Hummingbirds zip around the bushes. Past Balata, the winding road continues up into the Pitons du Carbet, a lush and fecund rainforest of ferns, bamboo and palms. Banana plantations cover the hillsides leading down to the coast.
Balata, 9km (5½ miles) north of Fort-de-France. Tel: (596) 64 48 73; www.jardindebalata.com. Open: daily 9am–5pm. Admission charge.

St-Pierre

Once the 'Paris of the Antilles', St-Pierre overlooks a splendid bay in the shadow of Mont Pelée. In the spring of 1902, after centuries of silence, Mont Pelée began to grumble. On 5 May, the volcano released a stream of mud and lava, but officials in the midst of an election campaign decided not to issue warnings. The governor arrived on 7 May, and urged people to leave, but only about 1,000 did.

Just before 8am on 8 May, the volcano erupted. A cloud of burning ash and poisonous gas at temperatures more than 2,000°C (3,700°F) swept over the town and into the sea where it caused the water to boil. Around 30,000 Pierrotins were asphyxiated. Miraculously, Auguste Cyparis, who was in the town's underground lock-up, survived.

St-Pierre never recovered, and its present-day population of 6,000 live among the gaunt reminders of the cataclysmic eruption. You can explore freely around the ruins of the theatre, Cyparis' cell and the rebuilt cathedral (only the façade survived). The before-and-after photographs in the **Musée Vulcanologique** are well worth a look. The Cyparis Express tourist train does the rounds of the sights if you don't feel like walking, though commentary is in French.
Musée Vulcanologique. Rue Victor Hugo. Tel: (596) 78 15 16. Open: daily 9am–5pm. Admission charge.

Musée Gauguin

The 19th-century French painter Paul Gauguin stayed on the beach here at Anse Turin for five months as he searched the Caribbean for a spot where he could live as a 'noble savage'. Reproductions of the paintings he produced in Martinique are on display.
Anse Turin, Carbet. Tel: (596) 78 22 66. Open: daily 9am–4.30pm. Admission charge.

Netherlands Antilles

The Dutch were important traders during the colonial era, and secured six possessions in the Caribbean: three in the Windward Islands and three in the Leewards. Sint Maarten in the Windwards is shared with France (see p124). The remaining Windward Islands, Saba and St Eustatius (known as 'Statia'), can only be visited by the very smallest cruise ships. Largely undeveloped, they remain rare oases of tranquility. More than 800km (500 miles) due south, the Dutch Leeward Islands of Bonaire, Curaçao and self-governing Aruba (the ABC islands) lie off the coast of Venezuela.

ARUBA

This low-lying, scrubby island, some 32km by 10km (20 miles by 6 miles), had inauspicious beginnings. It was claimed by Spain in 1499, but subsequently rejected as an *isla inútil* (useless island), and it was ignored for more than 100 years until the Dutch West Indies Company developed Curaçao. Aruba and neighbouring Bonaire proved useful for salt production and as ranches for cattle and horses. Few slaves were ever employed on the island, and it is therefore one of the rare places native Amerindians survived in situ, as can be witnessed in the faces of the local populace. The discovery of offshore oil in the 1920s led to an economic boom until declining prices turned the island towards tourism in the 1980s.

Though no longer technically a part of the Netherlands Antilles since gaining autonomy in 1986, Aruba

Netherlands Antilles

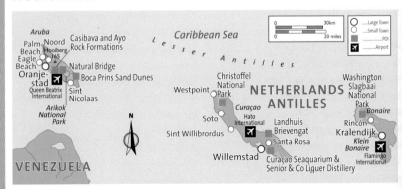

remains within the Kingdom of the Netherlands.

A taxi tour of the island takes just a couple of hours. Natural points of interest include the 165m (541ft) high **Hooiberg** (Haystack Hill) lookout point, and the Casibara and Ayo rock formations in the centre of the island.

On the north coast, the sea has carved the dramatic 30m (100ft) long, 8m (25ft) high coral rock **Natural Bridge** near Noordkaap, and there are huge dunes at **Boca Prins**. To the southeast, you can visit the ruins of the **Balashi Gold Mine** (some say the name 'Aruba' came from the Carib Indian words *ora uba* meaning 'gold was here'). You can also hike through the rugged surrounds of the **Arikok National Park** along well-marked trails. The most spectacular beaches, **Eagle** and **Palm**, edge the west coast north of Oranjestad.

Aruba Tourism Authority

PO Box 1019, 172 LG Smith Blvd, Oranjestad. Tel: (297) 582 3777; www.aruba.com. There's also a booth at the cruise ship terminal.

Arrival

Ships dock at the Port of Oranjestad terminal, which has shops and restaurants. The town centre is under ten minutes' walk away, but taxis line up next to the port. Fares are fixed, and drivers have copies of the official tariffs in their vehicles. Aruba's buses are fairly efficient, and you can reach most parts of the island from the central Oranjestad terminal.

Oranjestad

Behind a cordon of duty-free shopping malls, old town Oranjestad (pronounced Oran-yeh-stat) is fun to explore. Some of the best examples of Dutch Colonial architecture are found along Wilhelminastraat.

Overlooking the bay, 18th-century Fort Zoutman houses local history exhibits in the **Museo Arubano** (*Oranjestraat. Tel: (297) 582 6099. Open: Mon–Fri 8.30am–4.15pm. Admission charge*).

The **Archaeology Museum** displays Amerindian relics (*J E Irausquinplein 2A, near the post office. Tel: (297) 582 8969. Open: Mon–Fri 8am–noon & 1–4pm. Free admission*).

Dazzling white sands at Rodgers Beach, Aruba

BONAIRE

Like Saba and Statia, only small cruise ships visit Bonaire, docking at the terminal in the heart of the island capital, Kralendijk. Most visitors come here for the diving, which is among the best in the world. There's also duty-free shopping on Breedestraat, a 19th-century fortress, Fort Oranje, and the small **Bonaire Museum** ten minutes' walk east of town (*Kaya J van de Ree 7. Open: Mon–Fri 8am–noon & 1–5pm. Admission charge*). If you want to see the rest of the island, highlights include the salt pans in the south, home to many of Bonaire's 124 bird species; and the 9ha (22-acre) **Washington Slagbaai National Park** in the north, a former plantation site that's notable for its bird life and hiking trails. Taxis await ships at the port, and fares are set.

Tourism Corporation of Bonaire
Kaya Grandi 2, Kralendijk.
Tel: (599) 717 8322;
www.tourismbonaire.com

CURAÇAO

This is the largest of the Netherlands Antilles (measuring 61km by 14km/38 miles by 9 miles) with a fine natural harbour. The Dutch landed on Curaçao in 1634, and swiftly transformed the strategically placed island into a major trading centre for European and South American merchants. Curaçao flourished, attracting a polyglot community who in turn developed a bizarre local dialect, Papiamento, with strains of more than half a dozen European, South American and African tongues. To all appearances, Curaçao remains an exotic hybrid, a slice of picture-book Dutch in a spaghetti-Western setting, complete with cacti and tortured-looking *divi-divi* trees with branches forced back at 45 degrees due southwest by the cooling *Passatwinden* (tradewinds). Fans of the great outdoors should make for the arid but dramatic scenery of the Christoffel National Park.

Curaçao Tourism Development Bureau
PO Box 3266, Pietermaai 19, Willemstad. Tel: (5999) 434 8200; www.curacao-travel.com

Arrival

Cruise ships dock in the Otrabanda quarter, within walking distance of the town centre, the Punda, which is reached by the Queen Emma Bridge, from where you can easily explore the town on foot. (There is a free ferry when the bridge is open.) Taxis await the ships, and all are metred.

LANDHUIZEN

It is reckoned that there were around 300 plantations on Curaçao by the 19th century, most of them with a fine country house in the grounds. Eighty of these houses remain, of which around one-third have been restored. A real highlight of any trip to Curaçao is a visit to the 18th-century **Landhuis Brievengat**, just north of Willemstad. *Tel: (5999) 691 4961. Open: Mon–Fri 9.15am–noon & 3–6pm. Admission charge.*

Willemstad

The cruise ship visitor's introduction to Curaçao's capital, and one of the prettiest sights in the Caribbean, Willemstad's pastel-painted waterfront, the Handelskade, is a delight. It is said that a 19th-century governor first ordered the use of coloured paints on the red-roofed, gabled buildings as the dazzling whitewash was hurting his eyes. Today, it is a major tourist attraction.

Curaçao Museum

For a spot of island history, return to the Otrabanda district and the Curaçao Museum, which displays Amerindian and colonial relics in a restored former seamen's hospital.
Van Leeuwenhoekstraat. Tel: (5999) 462 3873. Open: Mon–Fri 8.30am–4.30pm, Sun 10am–4pm. Admission charge.

Curaçao Seaquarium

The wonders of the deep (and not-so-deep) are superbly displayed in picture-window tanks. Included are more than 400 varieties of local marine life, from fish to corals and sponges. Glass-bottomed boats sail out to the reef and there is a safe swimming beach here, too.
5.5km (3½ miles) east of Willemstad. Tel: (5999) 461 6666; www.curacao-sea-aquarium.com. Open: daily 8.30am–5.30pm. Admission charge.

Kurá Hulanda Museum

A beautifully put together collection of artefacts from Africa and South America, as well as a thoughtful and emotive exhibition on the trans-Atlantic slave trade. Audioguides give some background to the displays, and the shop sells a lovely selection of African art, CDs and musical instruments.
Klipstraat 9, Otrabanda. Tel: (5999) 434 7765; www.kurahulanda.com. Open: Tue–Sat 10am–5pm. Admission charge.

Christoffel National Park

This 1,820ha (4,500-acre) park was created from three old plantations in the northwestern corner of the island. It harbours native deer, iguanas and rare lizards as well as many of Curaçao's 500 different species of plants and flowers. Within the park four short trails for walkers and cars scale the sides of the Christoffelberg, Curaçao's highest hill at 378m (1,239ft). Guided tours are available.
Savonet, about 30km northwest of Willemstad. Tel: (5999) 864 0363. Open: Mon–Sat 7.30am–4pm, Sun 6am–3pm. Admission charge.

Bonaire slave huts, dismal and isolated

Puerto Rico

More than 1,600km (1,000 miles) southeast of Miami, Puerto Rico is the smallest of the four Greater Antilles islands, measuring around 177km by 56km (110 miles by 35 miles). Roughly rectangular in shape, it rises steeply from the developed coastal plains to a mountainous interior formed by the spine of the Cordillera Central, cloaked in lush tropical rainforest.

Arawak Indians called the island Borinquén, but Columbus rechristened it San Juan Bautista in 1493. Ponce de León, the discoverer of Florida, led the first group of Spanish settlers in 1508. He admired the *puerto rico* (rich port) of San Juan Bay and within a few years the island and the main settlement exchanged names. The Spanish held the island for 400 years, surviving hurricanes and frequent attacks by pirates and plunderers such as Sir Francis Drake, who sneaked past the town's defences to torch the Spanish fleet anchored in the harbour. Puerto Rican hopes for independence in the 19th century were dashed when Spain handed the island to the USA at the

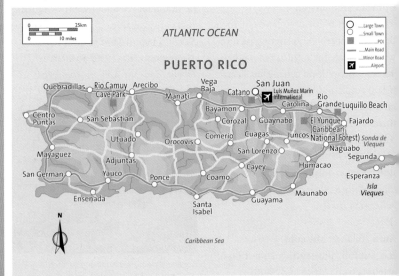

The massive fortifications of El Morro fortress in San Juan

end of the Spanish-American War in 1898. In 1917, USA citizenship was granted to Puerto Ricans, and the country is now a Commonwealth of the USA with an elected parliament run on the USA model.

The American influence is highly visible in the daily life of San Juan and in tourist areas, where English is widely spoken. Air-conditioned skyscrapers, chain hotels, gas-guzzling automobiles, American fashions, fast food and advertising are inescapable reminders of almost a century of US presence. However, the Puerto Ricans are proud and protective of their Latin origins. Catholicism, fiestas, the evening paseo (a pre-dinner stroll) and the clack of dominoes from bodegas and tapas bars lend Latin flavour to the streets of Old San Juan and quiet country villages.

Puerto Rico Tourism Company Information Center
La Casita, Calle Comercio, Old San Juan. Tel: (787) 722 1709;

www.gotopuertorico.com. There's also an information booth within the cruise ship terminal at San Juan.

Arrival

Ships dock at one of four cruise ship piers on the harbour in the heart of historic Old San Juan; from here you can see all the major sights on foot, though walking can be hard going given the fact that many of the streets wind their way up steep hills – you might want to take advantage of the free trolley-bus service. Taxis wait at all the cruise ship piers; all are metred for rides within San Juan, and fares are fixed to tourist sites further afield. The cruise ship docks are also within easy walking distance of the main bus station on Plaza de la Darsena, from where reliable government-run services operate around the greater San Juan area.

San Juan

The original Puerto Rico was well-named. It is now one of the world's top cruise destinations, home to more than 20 cruise ships which disgorge over a million passengers every year.

Old San Juan is a real slice of old colonial Spain with its pretty balconied houses painted in an array of pastel shades. Some streets are paved with blue-grey bricks transported as ballast in ships bound from Spain. On the return voyage, these same ships would be loaded with treasures plundered from South America.

The settlement was actually founded in 1520, and construction of the great El Morro fortress on the western peninsula began 20 years later. The growing town was enclosed by 9m (30ft) thick fortified walls punctuated by round stone sentry posts called *garitas*. The modern city has expanded beyond the walls; east along the Atlantic coast to the modern hotel and beach resorts of Condado and Isla Verde; south to the university district of Rio Piedras; and west around the bay to Catano, where the **Casa Bacardi Visitor Centre** offers tours and tastings of the famous rum (*Tel: (787) 788 8400; www.casabacardi.org. Open: Mon–Sat 8.30am–5.30pm, Sun 10am–5pm. Free admission*).

Within the compact Old Town area, the main shopping streets are Calle Fortaleza and Calle San Francisco, while a good place to find typical Spanish-style bars and restaurants is the area around Plaza de San José. The main sights are covered in the walk around Old San Juan (*see pp114–15*).

Fort San Cristóbal

At the northeastern corner of the Old Town, this imposing 17th-century fort sprawls over an 11ha (27-acre) site, bordered by five bastions fitted with cannons trained over the Atlantic approaches. There is an interesting scale model in the museum, and the Devil's Sentry Box is home to a resident spectral sentry.
Calle Norzagaray. Tel: (787) 729 6777.
Open: daily 9am–6pm.
Admission charge.

Museo de Nuestras Raíces Africanas

Fascinating museum dedicated to African history and culture as it has influenced Puerto Rican society. Arranged in chronological order, the nine rooms are packed with all manner of exhibits, from musical instruments to masks; there's also a detailed section on slavery that includes a replica of a Middle Passage slave ship.
Plaza de San José, San Sebastián St, Old San Juan. Tel: (787) 724 4294.
Open: Tue–Sat 9.40am–4.30pm.
Admission charge.

Museo de Arte

South of the Old Town, this is home to a huge collection of Puerto Rican art, with the works displayed chronologically, starting with paintings from the colonial era to modern pieces by the island's best known artists.
299 Avenida José de Diego, San Juan.
Tel: (787) 977 6277;
www.mapr.org.

Open: Tue & Thur–Sat 10am–5pm, Wed 10am–8pm, Sun 10am–6pm.
Admission charge.

Luquillo Beach

This magnificent stretch of golden sand on the eastern Atlantic coast sweeps around a bay lapped by inviting turquoise waters. There is plenty of shade beneath tropical palms, while beach bars sell fresh coconut milk, piña coladas, soft taco rolls filled with crab or lobster, alcapurrias (big banana fritters) and other delicious temptations. Quite simply – paradise!
Route 3, 48km (30 miles) east of San Juan.

Río Camuy Cave Park

A popular day trip, the Cave Park offers tours into a 52m (170ft) high

A waterfall in the rainforest of El Yunque

OLD TOWN TROLLEYS

A good way to get your bearings and see the sights is aboard the free, open-sided trolley buses that make narrated circuits of Old San Juan between 6.30am and 6.30pm. You can pick one up where you see the yellow *Parada* (stop) signs. There is a pick-up point outside the bus terminal, near the cruise-ship pier.

Puerto Rico

subterranean cavern adorned with monster stalagmites and stalactites. It is part of one of the biggest cave networks in the Americas, and there are views of the River Camuy, one of the world's largest underground rivers.
Route 129 (KM18.9), 80km (50 miles) west of San Juan.
Tel: (787) 898 3100.
Open: Wed–Sun 8am–4pm.
Admission charge.

El Yunque
(Caribbean National Forest)

More than 450 billion litres (100 billion gallons) of rainwater fall on El Yunque (The Anvil) every year, so be prepared. However, all this precipitation has created a spectacular, rampant rainforest containing over 240 native species, including vines, epiphytes, giant ferns and all manner of brilliant flowers. The El Portal Rainforest Centre, just off Route 191, has lots of background on park ecology.
Route 191, 64km (40 miles) east of San Juan. Tel: (788) 888 1810;
www.fs.fed.us/r8/caribbean.
Open: daily 7.30am–6pm.
Free admission.

Walk: Old San Juan

The best way to appreciate Old San Juan is on foot. In addition to the major sights, there are numerous pretty streets, houses bedecked with window boxes and decorative iron grilles, small museums and several welcoming refreshment stops.

Allow a minimum of 3 hours, with stops.

Start at La Casita.

1 La Casita

This pink house, formerly the Customs House, is now the tourist office.
Proceed down the Paseo de la Princesa below the Old Town walls.

2 Raíces Fountain

The Raíces Fountain overlooking the harbour pays homage to the Taíno, Indian (Arawak), Spanish and African influences on Puerto Rican culture.
Continue along the walls.

3 Puerta de San Juan

Re-enter the Old Town by this massive city gate. Its studded wooden door was built in 1635.
Turn left uphill to Plazuela de la Rogativa. Take the ramp on the right into the gardens. Paths cut up to Casa Blanca on the right.

4 Casa Blanca

The daughter and son-in-law of island founder Ponce de León built the original fortified house here in 1521,

which has been restored in period style and opened to visitors.
Tel: (787) 725 1454. Open: Tue–Sat 9am–noon & 1–4.20pm. Admission charge. Return through the gardens, and carry on up to the grassy headland and El Morro.

5 San Felipe del Morro

This stone fortress guards the entrance to San Juan Bay. It rises from the shore, with walls up to 6m (20ft) thick in places, and holds a maze of ramps and tunnels, lofty lookouts and dungeons. There are great views of the bay.
Tel: (787) 729 6754. Open: daily 9am–5pm. Admission charge. Walk back across the headland and bear left on Calle Norzagaray, past the Cuartel de Ballaja, the old Spanish barracks. Turn right up the steps of the Plaza del Quinto Centario.

6 Plaza de San José

A statue of Ponce de León stands on the square, but the real sight here is the

Iglesia de San José, a simple 16th-century church with a lavish altarpiece and monument to Ponce de León. Adjacent, the rickety Pablo Casals Museum displays cellos belonging to the famous musician.

Pablo Casals Museum. Tel: (787) 723 9185. Open: Tue–Sat 9.30am–5.30pm. Free admission. Head a short distance west on Calle San Sebastián, and look for the entrance to the narrow street of steps on the left.

7 Escalinatas

These attractive old streets made up of flights of steps are lined with beautifully restored pastel-painted town houses.

Turn left at the bottom of the first stepped street, then right down the next step street and left again at the bottom. Rejoin Calle Cristo by the 19th-century cathedral and turn right. Continue along Calle Cristo.

8 Capilla del Cristo

At the bottom of Calle Cristo, this tiny 18th-century chapel with gilded carvings, ornate silver altar and oil paintings celebrates the miraculous escape of a horseman saved by divine intervention as he was set to plunge off the cliff.

Open: Tue 11am–4.30pm. Free admission.

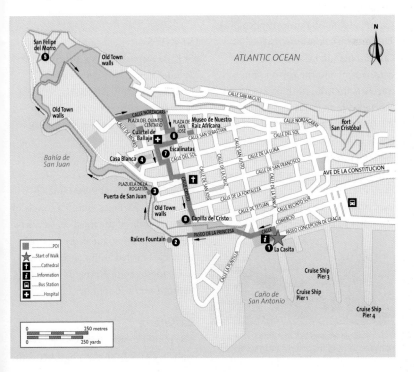

St Kitts and Nevis

This brace of volcanic Leewards Islands is separated by a 3km (2 mile) wide channel known as the Narrows. St Kitts is the larger of the two (at 176sq km/68sq miles), and is shaped like a tadpole, with the capital, Basseterre, on the southwest coast near the tail. A coast road circles the mountainous interior, dominated by Mount Liamuiga (1,156m/3,792ft), while another road runs down the tail, flanked on either side by white sand beaches.

The islands were sighted by Columbus in 1493, and he named the smaller one, Nevis, Nuestra Señora de las Nieves (Our Lady of the Snows) after its cloud-covered volcanic cone, which reminded him of a snow-capped peak. The larger island was christened St Christopher after Columbus' own patron saint and the patron saint of travellers. In time, both names were shortened to their present forms. In 1623, St Kitts was the first Caribbean island to be colonised by the English. And in 1626, in a rare (if brutish) display of common European purpose, English and French settlers massacred the Carib population at Bloody Point, a few miles west of Basseterre. Otherwise, the two colonialist powers fought intermittently for control of the islands' sugar industry until Britain gained the upper hand in 1783. St Kitts and Nevis achieved independence in 1983.

ST KITTS

St Kitts Department of Tourism

Pelican Mall, Bay Rd, Basseterre, St Kitts. Tel: (869) 465 4040; www.stkittstourism.kn. There's also an information centre at the cruise ship pier.

Arrival

Cruise ships dock at Port Zante of Basseterre's harbour, within a couple of minutes' walk of the town centre. Taxis meet all the ships, and rates are fixed with a list posted at the docks. Ferries to Charlestown in Nevis run from the harbour every 45 minutes.

Basseterre

The pint-size capital of St Kitts stretches back from the wharf between

Cannons point out to sea from the battlements of Brimstone Hill fortress

St Kitts and Nevis

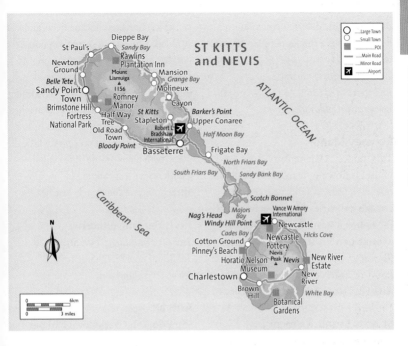

the twin poles of The Circus and Independence Square. Plumb in the centre of The Circus, a Victorian clock tower serves as a public meeting place, surrounded by colonial buildings, with stone ground floors topped by wooden upper storeys and laced with gingerbread detail. You might see the odd chicken strutting around grassy Independence Square, which is overlooked by the Catholic church and Georgian houses. For a glimpse of old-time Basseterre, browse through the photographs at the small **National Museum**, on Bay Street (*Tel: 869-465-5584. Open: Mon–Fri 9am–5pm, Sat 9am–1pm. Admission charge*).

Brimstone Hill Fortress National Park

Founded by the British in 1690, this colossal 15ha (37-acre) fortress crowns a 244m (800ft) peak. Once known as the 'Gibraltar of the West Indies' and now a UNESCO World Heritage Site, it was considered impregnable until 8,000 French troops managed to breach the 2m (7ft) thick Magazine Bastion walls after a month-long siege in 1782.

Main Rd, Brimstone Hill.
Tel: (869) 465 2609;
www.brimstonehillfortress.org.
Open: daily 9.30am–5.30pm.
Admission charge.

Rawlins Plantation Inn

Set in quiet countryside in the north of the island, this delectable plantation house hotel is a fine, quiet place to stop for lunch.

15km (9¼ miles) northwest of Basseterre. Tel: (869) 465 6221; www.rawlinsplantation.com

Romney Manor

This modest, 17th-century 'great house', is now home to Caribelle Batik, one of the island's most successful cottage industries. On the drive up to the house, a stone boulder features ancient Carib petroglyphs.

Tel: (869) 465 6253; www.caribellebatikstkitts.com. Open: Mon–Fri 9am–4pm. Free admission.

St Kitts Scenic Railway

Originally established to transport sugar cane from the fields to the factory, this quaint little narrow-gauge railway now takes visitors on the three-hour circular tour around the island (with some gaps filled in on buses), passing several key sights on the way, including Brimstone Hill and Mount Liamuiga, and crossing the 'Canyon Bridge'. Trips depart adjacent to the cruise ship pier and are available whenever there is a ship in port.

Tel: (869) 465 7263; www.stkittsscenicrailway.com. Admission charge.

NEVIS

The 'Queen of the Caribbees', Nevis was one of the most prosperous islands in the Caribbean during the 17th and 18th centuries. Carpeted in cane fields and studded with elegant plantation houses (*see box opposite*), it grew rich from the profits of its slave market and developed into a regular social whirligig, welcoming the likes of Horatio Nelson, who married local girl Frances (Fanny) Nisbet in 1787. Today, it's a quiet and very pretty little place, with a handsome little capital, Charlestown, a sprinkling of low-key attractions and four lovely beaches.

Nevis Tourism Authority

Treasury Building, Main Street. Tel: (866) 469 7550; www.nevisisland.com

Arrival

Ships dock in Charlestown harbour, but only the smallest can actually pull up at the dock; most have to anchor offshore and transport passengers in by tender to the ferry dock, right in the heart of the downtown area and within walking distance of all the town's points of interest. Taxis usually park around the ferry port when a ship is in dock, and you'll need one if you want to explore further than the town, such as to Pinney's beach. As they are not metred, fares must be agreed in advance.

Botanical Gardens

In the lee of the conical Nevis Peak, these charming gardens are dotted with sculptures and have areas devoted to roses, cacti, vines, bamboo and orchids.

PRINCESS CRUISES
escape completely

Wed. Fort Lauderdale

Thurs } at sea
Fri }

Sat Antigua

Sun St Lucia

Mon Barbados

Tues St Kitts

Wed St Thomas

Thurs at sea

Fri Princess Cays

Sat Fort Lauderdale

STAR PRINCESS

A replica great house holds the restaurant and souvenir shop.
Montpelier Estate, 3km (5 miles) south of Charlestown. Tel: (869) 469 3509. Open: Mon–Sat 9am–4.30pm. Admission charge.

Charlestown

The engagingly laid-back island capital (population 1,500) sports a riot of gingerbread decoration, a few craft shops and the interesting Alexander Hamilton House and Museum of Nevis History, set in the birthplace of 18th-century American statesman Alexander Hamilton, whose portrait still graces US$10 bills.
Main St. Tel: (869) 469 5786; www.nevis-nhcs.org/nevishistory.html. Open: Mon–Fri 8am–4pm, Sat 9am–noon. Admission charge.

Horatio Nelson Museum

A simple little museum near Charlestown's hot springs, and centred on Nelson himself, with everything from models of Nelson's Column in London to personal items owned by the great man. The outdoor springs, at a temperature of 40°C, are rich in minerals and said to be therapeutic.
5km/3miles east of Charlestown. Tel: (869) 469 0408. Open: Mon–Fri 8am–4pm, Sat 9am– noon. Admission charge.

New River Estate

Sugar production began at the 236ha (582-acre) New River plantation in the

PLANTERS' PARADISE

Many of the stately country houses built by rich Nevis sugar planters have been transformed into elegant hotels. If you feel like lunching in style, here are three suggestions:
Golden Rock Hotel: tropical forest setting with walking trails. *Tel: (869) 469 3346; www.golden-rock.com*
The Hermitage Inn: lovely antique-filled 18th-century house with terrace dining. *Tel: (869) 469 3477; www.hermitagenevis.com*
Montpelier Plantation Inn: beautifully restored stone house. *Tel: (869) 469 3462; www.montpeliernevis.com. Reservations advised.*

17th century and continued right up until 1956. You can stroll around the mill ruins, slowly disappearing beneath the undergrowth.
New River, 7km (4¼ miles) east of Charlestown.

Newcastle Pottery

Just past the Nisbet Plantation (now a very smart hotel), this roadside pottery workshop turns out simple handmade jugs, plant pots, candle shades and bowls decorated with bird and lizard figures made from local red clay.
Tel: (869) 469 9746. Mon–Fri 10am–4pm.

Pinney's Beach

Immediately north of Charlestown, Pinney's Beach continues south in a sweep of golden sand all the way to the ruins of Fort Ashby. Beach bars sell refreshments and snacks.

St Lucia

Arriving by ship is the best way to view St Lucia's famous Pitons, twin volcanic peaks which rise to a height of 732m (2,400ft) sheer out of the sea. The modern cruise-ship terminal, Pointe Seraphine, is a pleasant place to shop, but St Lucia's capital, Castries, is of limited interest. The best day trip options are to head north for the beaches and Pigeon Island, or take a tour of the south to see the Pitons and the so-called 'drive-in volcano' La Soufrière.

St Lucia is one of the loveliest of all the Caribbean islands. This did not escape the notice of the British and French who fought almost continually over the island between 1674 and 1814. The decisive battle was a bloody affair at Morne Fortune in 1796, though it was another 18 years before the French finally ceded St Lucia to the British. In 1979 the island gained independence.

St Lucia Tourist Board
Sureline Bldg, PO Box 221, Pointe Seraphine, Castries. Tel: (758) 452 4094; www.stlucia.org. There is also an information booth at the Pointe Seraphine complex.

Arrival

Ships dock at the Point Seraphine Cruise Ship complex, with restaurants and duty-free shops, on the northern side of the harbour, from where you can take a ten-minute walk the market and downtown area, or hop in a water taxi. If Seraphine is busy, they also dock across the harbour at Port Castries, close to the La Place Carenage duty-free shopping centre. Water taxis can also take you north to Rodney Bay beach and Pigeon Island, and taxis park up outside the docks to meet each ship. Some small ships anchor in Soufrière in the southwest; tenders bring you to shore, from where you can explore the town on foot. However you'll need a taxi to go further afield, such as to La Soufrière or the botanical gardens.

Taxis are unmetered, but a list of fares is posted at Point Seraphine and La Place Carenage.

Anse La Raye

Anse La Raye (it means 'Bay of the Rays' – stingrays in this case) is a typical fishing village of little wooden cottages and rusty tin roofs. The once plentiful rays have long since gone, but the fishermen are still here, with piles of nets and on the beachfront and boats bobbing in the bay. In the village

St Lucia

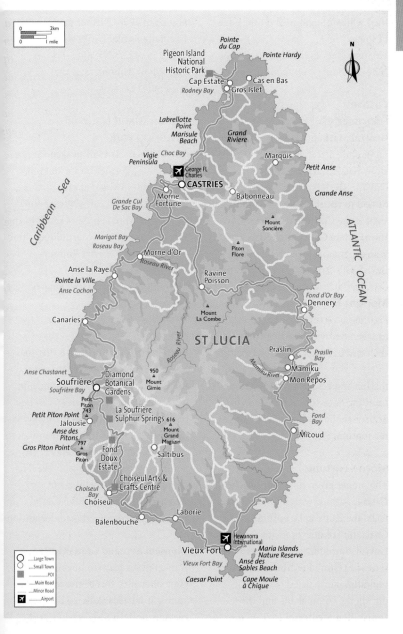

0   2km
0   1 mile

Pointe du Cap

Pointe Hardy

Pigeon Island National Historic Park

Cap Estate

Cas en Bas

Rodney Bay

Gros Islet

Labrellotte Point

Marisule Beach

Grand Riviere

Vigie Peninsula

Choc Bay

Marquis

Petit Anse

George FL Charles

CASTRIES

Babonneau

Grande Anse

Morne Fortune

Grande Cul De Sac Bay

Mount Soncière

Marigot Bay

Roseau Bay

Morne d'Or

Roseau River

Piton Flore

Anse la Raye

Pointe la Ville

Anse Cochon

Ravine Poisson

Fond d'Or Bay

Dennery

Canaries

Mount La Combe

ST LUCIA

Praslin

Praslin Bay

Anse Chastanet

Diamond Botanical Gardens

Soufrière

Soufrière Bay

Petit Piton 743

950 Mount Gimie

La Soufrière Sulphur Springs

616 Mount Grand Magazin

Mamiku

Mon Repos

Fond Bay

Petit Piton Point

Jalousie

Anse des Pitons

Gros Piton Point

797 Gros Piton

Fond Doux Estate

Saltibus

Micoud

Choiseul Arts & Crafts Centre

Choiseul Bay

Choiseul

Laborie

Balenbouche

Hewanorra International

Vieux Fort

Maria Islands Nature Reserve

Vieux Fort Bay

Anse des Sables Beach

Caesar Point

Cape Moule à Chique

Caribbean Sea

ATLANTIC OCEAN

N

O .....Large Town
O .....Small Town
■ .....POI
── .....Main Road
── .....Minor Road
✈ .....Airport

itself check out the murals decorating the church and playground walls; also the **La Sikwi Sugar Mill** on the edge of town.

La Sikwi. Tel (758) 452 6323. Open: Mon–Fri 8am–4pm. Admission charge.

Castries

For a flourish of local colour, visit **Central Market** (*Mon–Sat 8am–5pm*) on Jeremie Street. Covered stalls sell straw hats, local crafts and food. Outside, fresh fruit and vegetables spill out on to the sidewalk. The other main sight is the **Cathedral of the Immaculate Conception**, on Derek Walcott Square, the latter named for the island's famous Nobel Laureate.

Marigot Bay

Pretty as a picture, this bay has starred in several movies. Today, the idyllic sheltered harbour, encircled by steep forested slopes, plays host to a busy marina and resort. Take a water taxi from the dock to reach the beach, or browse the shops and cafés in the marina.

Morne Fortune

The jungle-green hill climbs up behind Castries, dotted with houses. At the peak, the landscaped grounds of Fort Charlotte are now home to the Arthur Lewis Community College, set in a series of restored red-brick military buildings constructed by the British during the colonial era, and the **Inniskillen Memorial** (*free admission*),

which commemorates the British fusiliers who captured the hill from the French in 1796. Further down, **Caribelle Batik** (*La Toc Rd. Tel: (758) 452 3785. Mon–Fri 9am–5pm*) demonstrates the ancient art of batik.

Pigeon Island National Historical Park

The distinctively twin-peaked Pigeon Island was a former pirate lookout, 18th-century British naval headquarters and early 20th-century whaling station. For views south to the **Pitons** and north to Martinique, climb up to the ruins of **Fort Rodney**.

Gros Islet, northwest coast. Tel: (758) 450 0603; www.slunatrust.org. Open: daily 9am–5pm. Admission charge.

Soufrière town and the Pitons

Soufrière is overlooked to the south by the towering bulk of Petit Piton, and some of the best Piton views can be enjoyed from the road as it runs down into town. (Gros Piton is three miles to the south.) A wander around Soufrière's main square will reveal its church and some gracious but weatherbeaten old buildings laced with intricate, faded gingerbread decoration.

Choiseul Arts and Crafts Centre

A marvellous place to buy unusual craft souvenirs, this centre teaches young St Lucians skills such as wood carving, pottery and weaving, and

many develop into first-class artists.
*Tel: (758) 459 3226. Open: Mon–Fri
8.30am–5pm.*

Diamond Mineral Baths and Botanical Gardens

Bring your swimsuit if you fancy a cure in these mineral baths, once enjoyed by Louis XVI's troops. The warm, milky-grey waters are fed by an underground spring from the Soufrière volcano and are said to have great restorative powers. The surrounding botanical gardens are lush and beautiful; at the Diamond waterfalls, the rockface and riverbed have been dyed orange by mineral deposits.
*Tel: (758) 459 7565;
www.diamondstlucia.com.
Open: daily 9am–5pm.
Admission charge.*

Fond Doux Estate

Just south of Soufrière, this 135-acre working plantation offers a lovely tour through its gardens, planted with flowers and local fruits. You'll also see the wonderfully rickety old buildings used to process the cocoa beans grown here, 95% of which are bought up by Hershey's chocolate manufacturers.
*Tel: (758) 459 7595;
www.fonddouxestate.com. Open: daily
8am–5pm. Admission charge.*

La Soufrière Sulphur Springs

You can drive most of the way up to La Soufrière's sinister and very smelly sulphur springs, then walk the final few yards to the bubbling pits. Guides point out the various coloured mineral deposits (green is copper oxide, purple is magnesium and so on), and add facts, figures and gruesome stories. There's also a museum centred on the area's geology.
*Tel: (758) 459 7686. Open: daily
9am–5pm. Admission charge. Continue
on around the southern coast.*

Southeast St Lucia

Just east of St Lucia's international airport, the white-sand Anse des Sables beach is the east coast's best and a centre for kite- and wind-surfing. Just offshore, the twin Maria Islands are home to a fascinating array of bird and plant life, and one has a small beach. The St Lucia National Trust offer guided visits.
*St Lucia National Trust. Tel: (758) 452
5005; www.slunatrust.org. Tour fee.*

Soufrière and the Piton mountains

St Martin/Sint Maarten

This tiny island, with an area of just 96sq km (37sq miles), is one of the most developed in the Caribbean. The French/Dutch division dates from 1648. Local lore has it that a Frenchman and a Dutchman set off in different directions around the island, and the dividing line would be drawn between the point of their departure and where they met up.

The Frenchman fared rather better, gaining a 54sq km (21sq mile) portion of the island for 'La Belle France'. The Dutch muttered darkly about wily French tactics (the strategic deployment of a nubile French maiden to delay their man), but eventually accepted the lesser portion.

Despite this dual arrangement, the two halves of the island get along well.

There are no internal border controls, and English is widely spoken. Most cruise ships anchor off the Dutch capital of Philipsburg, an attractive shopper's paradise. If you plan on visiting both sides of the island, head first for the French capital of Marigot, and enjoy coffee and croissants on the harbour before returning to bustling Philipsburg.

St Martin/Sint Maarten

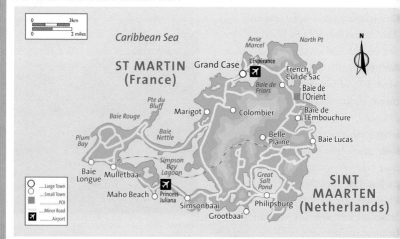

A CHOICE OF BEACHES

Both sides of the island boast good beaches, but the beaches on the (topless) French side are generally quieter with few facilities.

One of the best is **Baie Longue**, on the west coast, with its neighbours, **Plum Bay** and **Baie Rouge**, close runners-up. **Baie de l'Orient** on the northeast is equally lovely, and is the busiest beach on the French side, with beach bars and watersports.

Busy beaches with good facilities on the Dutch side include **Mulletbaai** (Mullet Bay), **Simsonbaai** (Simpson Bay) and **Grootbaai** (Great Bay Beach). At **Maho Beach** on the west side of the island, incoming jets swoop incredibly low over the sand as they land at the airport – quite a sight to behold, and one that's popular with photographers.

Office Municipal du Tourisme de St Martin

Route de Sandy Ground, Marigot Waterfront. Tel: (590) 875 721; www.st-martin.org

Sint Maarten Tourist Office

Vineyard Office Park, 106 Buncamper Rd, St Maarten N.A. Tel: (599) 542 2337; www.st-maarten.com

Arrival

Most ships dock at the A.C. Wathey pier, roughly 1.5km (1 mile) southeast of Philipsburg on the Dutch side of the island. From here, you can walk into town along the waterside boardwalk; otherwise, taxis await ships outside the pier, or you can also take a water taxi to Philipsburg's centre. Some ships anchor closer to the centre, and use tenders to bring passengers directly to Captain Hodge Pier, from where you can explore the city on foot. Taxis are unmetred, but fares are set by the government.

Marigot

Marigot is much more laid-back than its Dutch counterpart, with sidewalk cafés, faded colonial buildings and a colourful morning market on the waterfront. This is a great place to relax over a late breakfast and admire the harbour view, look around the French speciality stores, and maybe take a hike up to the ruins of the 18th-century **Fort St-Louis**.

Philipsburg

Philipsburg is the archetypal prettified West Indian town; its four main streets are intersected by *steegjes* (narrow alleys), painted in pastel colours and adorned with gingerbread woodwork. Front Street is a 16-block, open-air shopping centre, with a few fine old houses such as the lovely Pasangghran Royal Inn, a 19th-century former governor's residence, and the **Sint Maarten Museum**. The museum's displays of buttons, bones, old musket balls and other relics salvaged from HMS *Proselyte*, which sank in Grootbaai (Great Bay) in 1796, are of passing interest, but the house is an attraction in itself.

Sint Maarten Museum. 7 Front St. Tel: (599) 542 4917. Open: Mon–Fri 10am–4pm, Sat 10am–1pm. Admission charge.

St Vincent and the Grenadines

St Vincent and the 72km (45-mile) trail of tiny Grenadine islands stretching down towards Grenada is a top spot for Caribbean yachtsmen and other island hoppers. St Vincent is the largest of the islands at 344sq km (133sq miles), often referred to as 'the mainland' by the inhabitants of the 30 or so Grenadines, although many of these tiny cays are uninhabited.

St Vincent is explosively fertile – they say you could plant a pencil here and it would grow. The impenetrable green jungle barrier of the mountainous interior kept the Europeans at bay for years, and it provided excellent cover for warring bands of 'Yellow' (indigenous) and 'Black' (descended from runaway slaves) Carib Indians. After the Carib Wars ended in 1797, the British finally took control of the island, and established plantations of sugar cane, arrowroot and cotton.

St Vincent and the Grenadines Tourist Office
*Cruise-Ship Terminal, Bay St, Kingstown. Tel: (784) 457 1502; www.svgtourism.com
Bequia Tourism Association, Port Elizabeth, Bequia. Tel: (784) 458 3286; www.bequiatourism.com*

Arrival

Ships dock at the Cruise Ship Terminal, on the southeast side of the bay in Kingstown and within easy walking distance of the town centre. Taxis wait on the approach to the port when ships

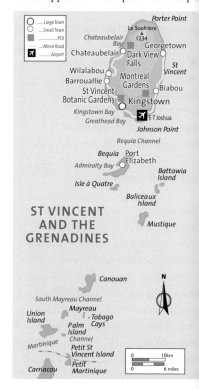

THE GRENADINES

Of the eight inhabited Grenadine islands, only two receive much in the way of visits from cruise ships.

Just 14km (8½ miles) south of St Vincent, smart little **Bequia** (pronounced Beck-way) is fronted by Port Elizabeth on Admiralty Bay. Diversions include good craft and T-shirt shops, several pleasant waterfront eating places, and water taxis to the lovely Princess Margaret and Lower Bay beaches.

The island of **Mayreau** (pronounced My-roo) makes Bequia look like a teeming metropolis. There are two wonderful beaches, or a steep hike up the hill to Dennis' Hideaway, where you can admire the view with one of Capt Dennis' lethal rum punches.

are moored but fares are not set, so negotiate an amount before you set out.

Kingstown

Behind the bustling waterfront, St Vincent's capital leads back into the steep hills that enclose the harbour. On Tyrrell Street, the marzipan yellow and white **St George's Cathedral** contains a memorial to Major Alexander Leith, who put down the Carib Rebellion of 1795. Tyrrell Street runs out of town up to Fort Charlotte, with sweeping views to the Grenadines, and inland to the island's volcanic vertebrae.

Around St Vincent

Northeast of Kingstown, the fertile **Mesopotamia Valley** is a veritable market garden, growing bananas, breadfruit, coconuts, cocoa, nutmeg, arrowroot and more. The **Montreal Gardens** here are stunning, with a riot of tropical flowers and plants wreathed through with paths.

Day trips head along the west coast to the lovely **Dark View Falls**. On the way you'll glimpse the foothills of **La Soufrière**, the landmark 1,234m (4,049ft), still-active volcano which dominates the northern sector of the island.

Montreal Gardens. Tel: (784) 458 1198. Open: 9am–5pm Mon–Fri, closed Sept–Nov. Admission charge.

St Vincent Botanic Gardens

Not to be missed, this is one of the oldest botanical gardens in the Western Hemisphere (founded 1765) and contains an amazing variety of weird and wonderful flora. Tip a guide to show you around oddities such as the sealing wax palm, the cannonball tree and the vast breadfruit tree, a descendant of the original plant brought to St Vincent by Captain Bligh in 1793.

Open: daily 6am–6pm. Free admission.

A walkway in St Vincent Botanic Gardens

Tortola and the British Virgin Islands

The Virgin Islands archipelago lies scattered across 2,590sq km (1,000sq miles) to the east of Puerto Rico. Less than 1.5km (1 mile) separates the westernmost of the British Virgin Islands (BVI) from its nearest US cousin, St John, but the dotted line on the map does more than divide British and US territory; it denotes a complete change of style. Tourism is relatively new in the 60-plus British islands, of which only 10 or so are populated. In fact, life is so laid-back you have to search pretty hard for a pulse.

The first visitors were Arawak and Carib Indians, followed by Christopher Columbus in 1493, who was so taken by the islands' beauty he named them after the 1,000 virgins in the legend of St Ursula. After Sir Francis Drake sailed through the channel between the two island groups in 1585, pirates and buccaneers found the islands an ideal hideaway. British planters introduced slave labour in the 18th century, but sailed away leaving the slaves behind. While other British islands sought independence in the 1960s, the BVI remained a Crown Colony. Economic ties with the US Virgin Islands (USVI) are strong (the US dollar is local currency), but for the time being, the inhabitants of the BVI are happy to remain separate and develop at their own pace, and are slowly becoming ever more popular with the yachting fraternity.

Tortola/British Virgin Islands Tourist Board
2nd Floor, Akara Bldg, De Castro St, Road Town. Tel: (284) 494 3134; www.bvitourism.com

Tortola

The largest of the BVI (18km by 5km/11 miles by 3 miles), Tortola is also the main destination for cruise ships, which anchor offshore of the capital, **Road Town**, and transport passengers to the Wickham's Cay yacht marina, from where it's a short walk into town. Road Town itself is a small place with displays on island history at the **Old Government House Museum** on Waterfront Drive (*Tel: (284) 494 4091. Open: Mon–Fri 9am–3pm, Sat 9am–2pm. Admission charge*), as well as the pretty **JR O'Neal Botanic Gardens** (*Tel: (284) 494 3904. Open: Mon–Sat 9.30am–5.30pm, Sun noon–5pm. Admission charge*).

Top of the island sights is **Sage Mountain National Park** at 523m (1,716ft), with fabulous views from the slopes of the high mountain, cloaked in primeval rainforest. Just north of here are lovely beaches at Cane Garden Bay and Apple Bay. You'll find taxis at Wickhams Cay and at the Road Town stand; all are unmetred, so make sure you agree on a fare before you set out.

Virgin Gorda

Virgin Gorda was 're-discovered' in the 1960s by Laurence Rockefeller, who built a luxury resort here at Little Dix Bay, the first of several elegant developments. The island also offers a selection of stunning coral sand beaches, the best of which are **The Baths**, a jumble of massive granite boulders forming grottoes and caves at the water's edge. Only the smallest ships anchor here, either at the capital, **Spanish Town**, just a short taxi ride from The Baths or in Leverick Bay and North Sound in the east and on the other side of the island from The Baths. Taxis are unmetred, so be sure to agree on a fare before setting out.

Virgin Islands

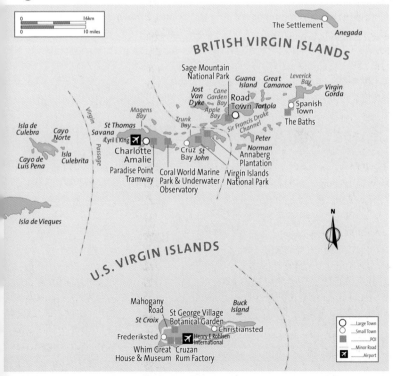

Trinidad and Tobago

A twin-island state, Trinidad and Tobago are like chalk and cheese. Trinidad is the larger of the two, at around 80km by 61km (50 miles by 38 miles), and is the biggest of the Lesser Antilles islands. Literally a chip off the block of South America, which occurred as recently as 10,000 years ago, Trinidad breaks from the traditional Caribbean island mould with an industrialised oil-based economy and an unusually diverse multiracial population.

Located just 32km (20 miles) away, Tobago (*see pp136–7*) is much more like its Windward Island neighbours. This tranquil, Caribbean idyll with its densely forested mountainous heart combines fishing and farming with a more developed, though nonetheless low-key, tourist industry concentrated on its beautiful beaches.

Trinidad and Tobago

The Arawak Indians' Iere (Land of the Hummingbird) was christened Trinidad (Trinity) by Columbus in 1498, after the three peaks which dominate its southern bay. A Spanish colony founded on the island in 1592 was destroyed (but not supplanted) by Sir Walter Raleigh in 1595, and thereafter the Spanish paid scant attention to Trinidad. French settlers introduced sugar and cocoa plantations towards the end of the 18th century, but Britain seized the island in 1797 and it was officially ceded to the Crown in 1802.

With the abolition of slavery in 1834, African slaves deserted the plantations and East Indian indentured labourers were shipped in to take their place. Between 1845 and 1917, some 145,000 Indians arrived in Trinidad and many stayed on after their five-year term of labour, so that Indians and Africans now each account for approximately 40 per cent of the population. Chinese cane field workers added further to the racial melting pot, and together with migrants from South America, Europe and the Middle East, constitute the remaining 20 per cent.

TRINIDAD
Arrival
In Trinidad, ships dock at the Cruise Ship Port on the waterfront in Port of Spain, within walking distance of Independence Square and the downtown area. Given the heat, you'll probably want a taxi if you're headed to the Savannah, National Museum or Zoo, though you can get to all three on foot in around half an hour. Taxis line up to meet ships on cruise ship days. As all vehicles are unmetred, make sure you agree on a fare before you set out.

Port of Spain
The hectic Trinidadian capital is the island in microcosm, a welter of modern skyscrapers and West Indian ginger-bread houses, pompous British colonial architecture, minarets and mosques.

On Frederick Street, markets and stalls sell everything from saris and bolts of Madras cotton to bootleg calypso CDs. Queen's Park Savannah is a huge, grassy breathing space with an eccentric collection of crumbling mansions nicknamed 'The Magnificent Seven'.

Botanical Gardens and Emperor Valley Zoo
These excellent gardens have spectacular flora and fauna.
200 Circular Rd. Tel: (868) 622 5343.
Open: daily 9am–6.30pm.
Admission charge.

Fort George
This fortress-cum-signal station was built in 1804. Fort George lies 20 minutes' drive from the centre of Port of Spain, above the St James suburb.

At 335m (1,100ft) above sea level it affords superb views over the island capital, and across to the mountains of northern Venezuela.

Queen's Royal College – one of the 'Magnificent Seven', Port of Spain

CARNIVAL

Introduced by French settlers during the 18th century, the Trinidad Carnival (or 'Mas' – short for masquerade) is one of the biggest street parties in the world.

Hundreds of thousands of Trinidadians and visitors, many of whom have crossed the world just to be here for the carnival, pack the streets of Port of Spain for the main competitions and parades which start on the Friday before Ash Wednesday.

It is a veritable sea of glittering costumes, with the dancers and devils, bird-men and butterfly-women sashaying and strutting to the rhythms of steel bands and soca music pumped from speaker-laden trucks.

The Trinidad Carnival is an almighty but well-organised free-for-all with competitions galore, culminating in the Parade of Bands (Monday and Tuesday), which proceeds noisily along Ariapita Avenue and the downtown area to the Queen's Park Savannah.

St James, Port of Spain. Open: daily 10am–6pm. Free admission.

National Museum and Art Gallery
An informative overview of Trinidadian history and culture, the museum tells the island's story through historical exhibits and artworks by local artists.
117 Frederick St. Tel: (868) 623 5941. Open: Tue–Sat 10am–6pm, Sun 2–6pm. Free admission.

Port of Spain environs
Asa Wright Nature Centre
A 'must' on any island tour, this nature centre was established in 1967 at the Spring Hill Estate on the edge of the rainforest. The old plantation house has been turned into a hotel so nature lovers

can stay up here and birdwatch from the balcony. Five trails lead off into the forest preserve which plays host to a stunning variety of native hummingbirds, butterflies, toucans and rare nocturnal oilbirds (or guacharos), once hunted by the Amerindians for their oil.

Near Arima, 20km (13 miles) east of Port of Spain. Tel: (868) 667 4655; www.asawright.org. Open: daily 9am–5pm. Admission charge.

Caroni Bird Sanctuary

This 182ha (450-acre) marsh, mangrove and lagoon sanctuary is home to the Trinidadian national bird, the scarlet ibis, as well as 157 other bird species, 80 types of fish, alligator-like caimans, sloths and great carpets of waterlilies. Tours are made by flat-bottomed boats, and the highlight (if time allows) is the spectacular dusk flight of ibises, who swoop down in large flocks to roost in the mangroves.

13km (8 miles) south of Port of Spain. Book via Nanan's Bird Sanctuary Tours. Tel: (868) 645 1305; www. nananecotours.com. Admission charge.

Chaguaramas Peninsula

Leased to the American military during World War II, this peninsula is now protected as part of the Chaguaramas National Park. Of the clutch of islands just off the western end of the peninsula, **Gaspare Grande** boasts a cave complex adorned with stalactites and stalagmites. Another diversion on the mainland is the **Military History**

Museum, a ramshackle but engaging collection of artefacts that gives insight into the American occupation (*Open: daily 9am–5pm. Admission charge*).

10km (7 miles) northwest of Port of Spain.

Maracas Bay

The road north from Port of Spain, known as Saddle Road, cuts a scenic roller-coaster route through to the coast. There are superb views along the way, and the magnificent palm-fringed sandy beach at Maracas Bay is a popular spot at weekends, with changing facilities and stalls selling shark and bake, shark-meat in fried bread served with salad and spicy sauces.

29km (18 miles) north of Port of Spain.

Further afield

Pitch Lake

Worth a mention, though probably not practical for day trippers (it is a six-

(*Cont. on p136*)

Maracas Bay boasts one of Trinidad's best beaches

Calypso

Music is the heartbeat of the Caribbean, and alongside Jamaican reggae, T&T's calypso and steel pan have become synonymous with the region's musical output. Trinidad is the home of calypso, where it was first recorded in the 19th century, but its roots lie buried deep in the West African oral tradition of the griot, a travelling musician who brought news and gossip from village to village via song. During the slave era, Africans were forbidden to speak in their native tongues, but singing was permitted as a means of making work on the plantations more bearable. This chink in the planter's 'seasoning' process (see pp14–15) was swiftly turned into a means of keeping African story-telling traditions alive. Many of the songs had an allegorical slant, using animals or birds to hide real identities, and as such they were both protest songs and a way of passing on information. The word 'calypso' is though to be derived from the West African *kai-so*, an expression of encouragement or approval.

Protest and gossip laced with humour are still the cornerstones of calypso today. The basic two-four or four-four rhythm does not permit an immense range of melodies, but

calypso is strongly judged on its lyrical content, and its exponents are hailed as poet-performers in the West African troubadour tradition.

Calypsonians pull no punches. Their subject matter covers the spectrum from love, life and politics, to cricket or baldly stated warnings about AIDS, while styles vary from belligerent to raucous or downright raunchy. In competitions, other opponents are considered fair game and can be demolished with a few swipes of wickedly barbed humour.

The big names in calypso are partial to some pretty grandiose titles themselves: Lord Nelson and Lord Kitchener, Attila the Hun and the Black Stalin, among them. Perhaps the biggest of them all, the Mighty Sparrow's career has spanned more than 30 years, and he has more Calypso Monarch (the top Trinidad Carnival calypso award) titles to his name than any other. Although calypso was largely a male preserve in its early days, the success of Calypso Rose (Rose Lewis), who in 1978 became the first woman to win the Monarch competition, paved the way for many more female performers, from Singing Sandra to Denise Plummer. These days, though, calypso

Steel drums are the main instrument used in calypso

takes something of a backseat to soca, its faster, more dance-oriented young cousin – and it's soca that you'll hear blasting through the streets at Carnival time.

But even more evocative of the Caribbean is the sound of the steel pan, which was invented in Trinidad in the 1930s, when enterprising musicians stretched and tempered the lids of oil drums which had been discarded by the oil industry to create a brand new instrument. First played in the poorest sections of Port of Spain, the sound grew in popularity and soon became the street music of Carnival, initially as a small 'pan around the neck' group of players, and now as 300-strong bands who tour the parade route with their instruments loaded on to a converted flatbed.

hour round-trip from Port of Spain), this 36ha (90-acre) asphalt 'lake' is a truly bizarre natural phenomenon and one of the largest deposits of its kind in the world. It is said Sir Walter Raleigh caulked his ships with the black tar which seeps through the earth's crust and forms a bouncy skin which you can walk on. Around 91m (300ft) deep at its centre, the level of the lake is slowly dropping as the tar is mined for sale around the world.

60km (40 miles) southwest of Port of Spain.

TOBAGO

Trinidad's little sister makes a virtue of being different. Tobago is smaller, but prettier. The sedate lifestyle is so much more relaxing – perfect for holiday-makers who want to unwind – and there is little crime. Whereas Trinidadians tend to write off Tobagonians as being rather unsophisticated (though they still love to come here for weekend breaks), the people of Tobago pride themselves on being friendlier and more welcoming than the street-sharp 'Trickidadians'.

Trinidad and Tobago's political links originated fairly recently. A former pirate enclave turned prosperous sugar island, Tobago was grouped and governed with the Windward Islands until the late 19th century when the sugar industry collapsed. The island went bankrupt and was appended to up-and-coming Trinidad. Poor and underdeveloped, relying on subsistence agriculture for much of this century, Tobago has been rescued by the emergent tourism industry, which remains relatively low-key. The island's chief charms include unspoilt tropical forests and excellent snorkelling.

Arrival

In Tobago, ships moor up at the Scarborough Port, which has a surrounding complex of shops. From here, you can easily walk to the market and Botanical Gardens, but you'll need a taxi to get to the beaches and other attractions. Taxis park up just outside the terminal, and a list of set fares is posted just inside.

Scarborough

A bustling little split-level town with a small cruise ship complex, Scarborough is the island capital. Just inland of the harbour, there is a colourful market, and the **Botanic Gardens** are a short walk away (*Open: daily 6am–6pm. Free admission*). Further uphill,

---

ROBINSON CRUSOE

Stop for a chat in Tobago and you might be regaled with tales of the island's favourite character, the shipwrecked mariner of Daniel Defoe's novel *Robinson Crusoe*.

Published in 1719, Defoe's novel was based on the real-life exploits of a mariner, Alexander Selkirk, who was shipwrecked in the Pacific, off the coast of Chile. But Defoe moved his hero to Tobago. The Tobagonians, in turn, have adopted Crusoe, and even named a cave on the northwest coast after him.

remnants of the colonial era include the 1825 House of Assembly and Gun Bridge, with railings made from recycled rifle barrels.

Argyle Falls

Tobago's most visited waterfall, and the island's highest, at 54m (177ft) high, Argyle is reached via a gentle 15-minute walk from the main road. There's a deep pool for swimming at the bottom, and you can climb the three tiers to the top.
Windward Rd. Tel: (868) 660 4154.
Open: daily 9am–4pm.
Admission charge.

Fort King George

Perched on the hilltop 131m (430ft) above town, this 18th-century British fortress makes a terrific lookout point with views along the island's Windward coast and over to Trinidad on clear days. It now houses a small, but informative, museum of Amerindian and colonial artefacts in the Barrack Guard House.
Open site. Free admission.
Museum. Open: Mon–Fri 9am–4.30pm.
Admission charge.

Pigeon Point

This is the classic Caribbean beach, a strand of powder-soft white sand fringed with palms. There are snack bars, changing facilities, watersports and glass-bottomed boat trips out to the superb **Buccoo Reef National Park**.

Open: daily 8am–dusk. Admission charge.

Tobago Forest Reserve

Another favourite spot for nature lovers, the Tobago Forest Reserve is the oldest of its kind in the Western Hemisphere, set aside by the British in 1764. Near Bloody Bay Lookout Site, the Main Ridge Forest Trail begins its winding descent through the rainforest to Bloody Bay, named after a gory ancient battle when the sand and sea turned red with spilled blood. Tropical birds and large, brilliant butterflies dazzle beneath the forest canopy and guides lead walks along the trails from Gilpin Trace.
Set above the northwest coast, near Parlatuvier.

Clear water, white sand and natural shade, if desired, on Pigeon Point Beach

Trinidad and Tobago

US Virgin Islands

The 'American Paradise', the US Virgin Islands are a collection of some 50 islands and cays east of Puerto Rico. The three main islands are St Thomas and St John in the north, and St Croix (pronounced 'Croy'), out on a limb, some 64km (40 miles) due south. The American influence is all-pervasive in St Croix and St Thomas, two of the most developed islands in the Caribbean. St John is an exception since two-thirds of its 41sq km (16sq miles) is a protected national park. (See map on p129.)

Christopher Columbus anchored off St Croix on 13 November 1493 on his second voyage to the New World. The following day he set sail for the lands visible on the northern horizon, and spent four days charting the jumble of islands he named Las Once Mil Virgenes (the 11,000 Virgins). The Spanish tried to settle St Croix shortly afterwards, but it was abandoned for over a century. Dutch, English and French colonists arrived next in 1625, but were ousted by the Spanish in 1650, who in turn were almost immediately evicted by the French.

Meanwhile, the Danish West Indies Company set up a permanent base on St Thomas in 1671, claimed St John in 1684, and set to work planting sugar cane, cotton and indigo estates. St Croix was bought from the French in 1733.

St Thomas was declared a free port in 1724, and profited handsomely from the European conflicts being fought in the Caribbean. During the American War of Independence, Danish neutrality and St Thomas' free port status initiated strong ties with the USA. An early attempt by the USA to buy the islands from the Danes in 1867 was vetoed by the islanders but in 1917, the collapse of the sugar trade finally persuaded the islands' inhabitants to opt for the USA bid.

ST CROIX

The largest of the Virgin Islands (212sq km/82sq miles), St Croix is far behind St Thomas in the tourist development stakes, and this is part of its charm. There are fewer crowds and the locals have more time to chat, and it's a much more relaxing experience overall, with a charming capital, **Christiansted**. If you have time, take a drive through the 6ha (15-acre) patch of semi-rainforest, east of the island's other main settlement, **Frederiksted**, and bisected by the Mahogany Road. Trails and vehicle tracks criss-cross beneath 30m (100ft) tall mahogany trees surrounded by lush ferns and invaded by bromeliads.

USVI/St Croix Tourist Office

PO Box 4538, 41A Queens Cross St, Christiansted, 00822–4538 USVI. Tel: (340) 773 0495; www.usvitourism.vi. There's also an information booth at the Frederiksted pier.

Arrival

Ships dock at the Anne Abramsom cruise ship port at Frederiksted, a quiet little town on the west coast, 27km (17 miles) from Christiansted. From the port, you can easily explore Frederiksted on foot, but to get to Christiansted and other attractions around the island, you'll need a taxi. Taxis await ships at the port, but all are unmetered, so you must settle on a fare before you drive away or ask to check the list of government rates that drivers carry. Government-run buses also shuttle regularly between the port and Christiansted, and are a less expensive option, but services around the rest of the island are a little unpredictable.

Christiansted

A delightful small port settlement set back from the harbour and toy-town Fort Christiansvaern, Christiansted offers good shopping and some great little restaurants and bars. The settlement was originally founded in 1735, and there are still several 18th- and 19th-century buildings dotted about. The most notable of these is the **Steeple Building**, a former Lutheran church which now houses a modest museum dedicated to the island's national park, with natural history displays (*Open: daily 8am–4.30pm. Free admission*).

Offshore to the east of Christiansted, the 344ha (850-acre) **Buck Island Reef National Monument** offers the best beach on (or rather off) the island, with two underwater snorkelling trails and excellent snorkelling and diving. Frequent boat services for the island leave from the docks in Christiansted.

US Virgin Islands

Yachts off Caneel Bay, on the northwest coast of St John, US Virgin Islands

Trunk Bay, St John, is rated one of the top ten beaches in the world

Fort Christiansvaern

Bearing more than a passing resemblance to a rather large toy castle, this yellow and white fortress was largely completed between 1738 and 1749. It has been restored to its appearance circa 1830–40, with neat, green painted shutters and pyramids of cannon balls.
Tel: (340) 773 1460; www.nps.gov/chri. Open: daily 8am–4.45pm. Admission charge.

Cruzan Rum Factory

A favourite stop on the tourist trail in the western corner of the island, this modern factory was built in the grounds of the former Diamond Sugar Mill. Half-hour tours trace the distilling process, followed by tastings.
Off Centerline Rd, near the airport. Tel: (340) 692 2280; www.cruzanrum.com. Open: Mon–Fri 9–11.30am & 1–4.15pm.

Frederiksted

With pretty stone arcades topped with gingerbread decoration protecting passers-by from the sun's glare, St Croix's second town, Frederiksted, runs along two streets from blood-red Fort Frederik at the waterfront. Dating back to 1760, the fort was destroyed by fire in 1878, and restored in Victorian style. It now houses a well-displayed and informative museum covering island history and culture, with a good section on hurricanes. In 1776, the new American flag received its first foreign salute from the cannons of Fort Frederik.
Fort Frederik. Tel: (340) 772 2021. Open: Mon–Fri 8.30am–4pm. Donations accepted.

Caribbean Museum Centre for the Arts

An interesting little museum established to promote the art and artists of the USVI. The exhibitions change regularly, and include some interestingly quirky work, a world away from the usual watercolours in tropical hues.

10 Strand St. Tel: (340) 772 2622; www.cmcarts.org. Open: Wed–Sat 10am–4pm. Free admission.

St George Village Botanical Garden

On a 6.5ha (16-acre) site where Arawak Indians once set up camp and the Danes operated a sugar mill from 1733 to 1917, this botanical garden showcases more than 1500 species of tropical plants. There is plenty to admire, including orchid and fern houses, a fragrant frangipani walk and a rainforest trail.

Centerline Rd, near Frederiksted. Tel: (340) 692 2874; www.sgvbg.org. Open: Mon–Sat 10am–4pm. Admission charge.

Whim Great House and Museum

Don't miss this gracious, 18th-century house with 1m (3ft) thick walls and an air moat designed to keep the cellar cool. The unusual oval-shaped interior has been restored with period colonial furnishings and paintings. In the grounds, the sugar estate's old windmill and cane crushers can be seen.

Centerline Rd. Tel: (340) 772 0598; www.stcroixlandmarks.com. Open: guided tours Mon–Sat 10am–4pm. Admission charge.

ST JOHN

A short boat ride from St Thomas, St John is one of the best-preserved islands in the Caribbean. In 1956, two-thirds of the island was given by owner Laurence Rockefeller to the National Parks Service, since when the land-based portion of the 5,220ha (12,900-acre) preserve has been returned to its natural forest state. Around 2,265ha (5,600 acres) of the park lie under water off the north coast. Most visitors to the island are day trippers; there are frequent daily ferry sailings from Charlotte Amalie and Red Hook (St Thomas) to Cruz Bay. Almost all cruise ships are too large to dock here; instead, they anchor off Cruz Bay and transport visitors to the ferry dock by tender. The visitors' centre near the dock has information about the park and its 22 walking trails, which range from 10 minutes to a couple of hours in length. The **Estate Annaberg Plantation** ruins on the central north coast are one of the park's highlights. St John's best beaches are in the north. **Trunk Bay**, rated among National Geographic's top ten

Cruz Bay, St John

beaches, has snack facilities, snorkel hire and an underwater trail.
Virgin Islands National Park.
Tel: (340) 776 6201; www.nps.gov/viis

ST THOMAS

When Dutch planters and the Danish West India Company first set up shop on St Thomas in the 1670s, the harbour settlement outside the walls of Fort Christian was known as Taphus, literally 'tap house', and it was a welcome watering hole for Caribbean merchants. Taphus was rechristened Charlotte Amalie in 1691, in honour of the Danish queen. Before long, the dockside waterhouses were piled high with goods from around the world, a tradition which has continued right through to the present day – though rather than rum, guns, indigo and cotton, the contents are now French perfumes and designer watches, shipped in to the duty-free stores that serve the millions of cruise-ship passengers who visit annually.

St Thomas Tourism Division Visitors' Bureau

78 Contant, Elaine Co Building 1-2-3, Charlotte Amalie, 00802 USVI.
Tel: (340) 774 8784; www.usvitourism.vi.
There's also an information office at Havensight Mall.

Arrival

Ships dock either at the Havensight Mall, 2.5km (1.5 miles) southeast of Charlotte Amalie town centre or at the Crown Bay Marina, around 4km (2½ miles) to the west of the town. Walking into the centre from either isn't very pleasant; taxis wait at both docks when ships are in port. All are unmetred, so do settle on a fare with the driver before you set out.

Charlotte Amalie

A pretty waterfront town clambering back into the hills from the mercantile mayhem on Main Street, Charlotte Amalie is a major cruise ship destination, servicing up to ten ships a day. The downtown area is a shrine to duty-free shopping, but if you prefer a breath of fresh air, and a taste of the town's history, take a stroll up Government Hill to explore the quiet streets of 19th-century public buildings and hotels linked by flights of steps.

Blackbeard's Castle

Attractively lined with palm trees and built with bricks used as ballast on Dutch trading ships, the so-called '99 Steps' (there are actually 103 of them) lead up to the commanding lookout point known as Blackbeard's Castle. Local legend claims the ferocious pirate maintained a base on the island in the 1690s and early 1700s, using the tower as a lookout point to track passing ships (and potential plunder). His days of lacing rum with gunpowder and splicing his beard with burning charges before going into battle ended when his ship, the *Queen Anne's Revenge*, was captured by Lieutenant Robert Maynard of the Royal Navy in 1718, and Blackbeard was killed in the fight.

Coral World Marine Park and Underwater Observatory

An alternative introduction to the marine world, this small but effective complex features a 365,000-litre (80,000-gallon) reef tank and 'predator' tanks, as well as an underwater observatory over a living reef 100 feet out into the ocean. There's also a stingray lagoon, turtle pool and regular fish feeding sessions and the chance to swim with sea lions. The park also offers changing facilities and showers for visitors who want to relax on neighbouring Coki Beach, which also offers fantastic snorkelling.
4km (2½ miles) northeast of Charlotte Amalie. Tel: (340) 775 1555; www.coralworldvi.com. Open: daily 9am–5pm. Admission charge.

Magens Bay

This fabulous beach boasts over 1.5km (1 mile) of talcum powder sand sandwiched between serried ranks of palm trees and limpid blue water. It features in National Geographic's list of top ten beaches in the world (along with Trunk Bay on St John).
5km (3 miles) north of Charlotte Amalie. Admission charge.

Paradise Point Tramway

A great way to get a panoramic view of the town centre, the harbour and the offshore islands, these cable-car trams take you up Flag Hill to Paradise Point, where there are nature trails and bird shows.
9617 Estate St. Tel: (340) 774 9809; www.paradisepointtramway.com. Open: Thur–Mon 9am–5pm, Tue 9am–8pm, Wed 9am–9pm. Admission charge.

St Peter Great House and Botanical Gardens

The outstanding feature of this contemporary great house is its fabulous views. From the observation deck at 305m (1,000ft) above sea level you can see 20 other islands. Take a stroll around the gardens, where more than 500 varieties of plants flourish.
3km (2 miles) north of Charlotte Amalie. St Peter Mount Rd. Tel: (340) 774 4999; www.greathouse-mountaintop.com. Open: Mon–Sat 8am–4pm. Admission charge.

The Frederick Evangelical Lutheran Church on Government Hill, Charlotte Amalie

When to go

Most people visit the Caribbean to escape the cold of winter in the northern hemisphere, and cruisers are no exception, with the vast majority of passengers setting sail during the mid-November to mid-April high season. During this time, you'll have more choice in terms of routes, while on the islands, all the restaurants, shops, bars and attractions will be open, and the weather is at its most delicious: hot and sunny during the day, and pleasantly cool in the evenings.

Though the summer sun can be blistering throughout the region, and you'll also risk high humidity and the odd shower of rain, summer is the next busiest time, with families taking advantage of the school holidays.

The slowest time of year in the Caribbean cruise calendar are the months of September, October and early November. During this low season, the likelihood of a hurricane is at its highest, and rainfall is more frequent than at any other time of the year. The unpredictable weather, however, means that it's a buyers' market and you can pick up some excellent cruise deals; and the islands themselves are a lot less busy, making for a more laid-back experience.

Whatever time of year you take your cruise, however, you will get some sunshine – guaranteed – and daytime temperatures that range from 25°C to 33°C. And even if it rains, it'll usually just be a tumultuous tropical downpour: dramatically heavy, but mercifully brief.

HURRICANES

June – *too soon*
July – *stand by*
August – *prepare you must*
September – *remember*
October – *all over*
Traditional Caribbean hurricane season rhyme

Mention hurricane season in the Caribbean, and many people – locals and visitors alike – will give a hearty shudder. But although the region is something of a hurricane hotspot, big blows are no more likely here than they are in Miami or the Gulf Coast, and the chances of you sailing through a hurricane while on a cruise are tiny – satellite tracking can pick up a big storm far in advance, giving the ships time to move out of the predicted path. This may mean missing a stop on an island in the cruise itinerary, or even switching from an Eastern Caribbean route to a Western Caribbean one, so if you cruise in the official hurricane season months (June 1 to November 30), it's best to be prepared for this possibility. Bear in mind, also, that outrunning a storm may mean a couple of days of rough seas, and a little more rain than you'd hoped for. If you want to track any storms in the region, the United States National Hurricane Centre website (*www.nhc.noaa.gov*) has comprehensive information on all weather systems that threaten the region.

Cruises around the Caribbean have been a popular way of touring the scenic islands for decades

Getting around

Though many cruise-ship passengers prefer to see their ports of call on a tour organized by the cruise line, others want to explore independently.

Caribbean cruise ship docks are often conveniently located just steps away from the heart of the island's capital, but in other ports, the action is a little further away. As walking any distance in the blazing heat of a Caribbean morning can be an exhausting experience, you may well opt to be transported to your destination. Renting a car can be a fraught experience when you've only a few hours to see each island; equally, many islands require you to buy a temporary driving license to get behind the wheel, which will bump up the cost of a car by at least US$20. For these reasons, car rental is not generally convenient or cost effective for cruisers, and details of rental outlets haven't been included in this guide.

Taxis

Taxis are by far the most convenient and popular way for cruise-ship passengers to explore their ports of call. Licensed taxis (usually sporting formal identification either in the form of an ID badge on the driver, or an official sticker in their vehicle) invariably line up outside the port when a ship is in dock. As well as taking you from A to B, taxis are a great way to tour the islands; most drivers will double up as guides, pointing out the sights and giving a little informed background to the things you see. And as they work regularly with cruise ships, they can also help plan an efficient tour route than enables you to see everything you're interested in and get back to the ship on time. Hiring a driver for the day can work out expensive, however, so you may want to club together with some other passengers – conveniently, licensed drivers in many ports have minivans rather than regular cars. Equally, you don't have to set out for a full day of touring; you could explore on foot in the morning, and hit the road after lunch. Similarly, you might want to just head for the island's must-see beach or prime attraction.

As to prices, things vary enormously from island to island. In some, you'll find metred taxis; in many others, fares are regulated by the government, with a sample list displayed at the port or carried in each vehicle. And in others it's simply a matter of agreeing on a price with the driver – something you'll also have to do if you book a sightseeing tour rather than a straight journey. In all cases, settle the amount before you set out; and if you want to deviate from your agreed route along the way, ask the price first.

Buses

As public transport in the Caribbean can leave a lot to be desired, only the more adventurous of cruisers tend to use buses. Though some islands boast shiny air-conditioned fleets owned and operated by the government (we've noted these instances in the individual destination guides), the vast majority have a bus service that's ad-hoc to say the least. 'Buses' are usually minibuses which ply loosely set routes, leaving their point of embarkation (usually a bustling terminus in the capital) only when jammed full, and then screaming along the roads at breakneck speed. They stop wherever their passengers want (they'll also pick you up in any location, too – just stick out your arm), and fares are very cheap. The downside is that there are no schedules, so while you may be able to get to your destination easily enough, you can't be

sure of a bus to get you back before the ship leaves. For this reason, buses are only really worth considering for short hops – from a far-flung docking area to the town centre, for example – or on islands small enough that you're never going to be too far away from your ship, such as St John in the US Virgin Islands. If you do use buses, it's better to pay with local currency rather than US dollars; you pay the driver or conductor (the man with a wad of notes), and just call out when you want to get off.

A masted cruise ship in port on the US Virgin Islands

Food and drink

Caribbean cooking has few pretensions, but many influences: African-inspired pepperpot stews, cornmeal fungee or okra-filled callaloo soup, Indian curries in Trinidad and beyond and delicately spiced Creole fare in the French islands. And, wherever you go, the seafood is always delicious, whether it's lobster in classic garlic butter or simple steamed fish.

Though Caribbean cooking varies wildly from island to island, something that all the countries have in common is the produce, much of which was first brought to the region by Africans during the plantation era; one exception is breadfruit, which arrived in the Caribbean on Captain Bligh's ill-fabled *Bounty*, and was imported in order to serve as a cheap food to feed slaves. It's still a staple side dish, served baked, fried or in flavoursome breadfruit balls or gratins. Other common accompaniments, often called ground provisions, are dense tubers such as yam, tannia, eddoe and purple-tinged dasheen; as well as fried ripe or green plantains. Callaloo (leaves of the dasheen plant in Trinidad, and a more spinach-like plane in Jamaica) is a popular green vegetable, cooked with onions, garlic and okra. And, whenever you go, you'll find a take on rice and peas, rice cooked with coconut milk and pulses (called peas here) such as kidney beans or pigeon/gungo peas.

Originating in Jamaica but now available throughout the Caribbean, jerk is always delicious – chicken, pork and sometimes sausage or fish marinated in special spices and cooked over an aromatic barbecue of pimento wood. Another ubiquitous lunchtime filler is the roti, a wheat 'skin' wrapped around curried meat and vegetables. The best rotis are in Trinidad, where the skins come filled with ground split peas, but you'll find more basic versions across the Eastern Caribbean. Another staple is rice and a chicken dish cooked in coconut milk; *arroz con pollo* in Puerto Rico, or pelau in Trinidad. Other specialities to look out for include Grenadian oildown, a selection of fresh and salted meat cooked with coconut milk; and cornmeal dishes such as fungee (a gloopy Antiguan mix with okra) or coocoo, cooked solid and sliced as a side dish in Barbados. Pepperpot soup, meanwhile, is a delicious blend of callaloo, pumpkin and salt pork; some islands include beef in the mix.

There is plenty of fresh seafood including lobster, shrimp, crab, flying fish (excellent in a sandwich) and conch (pronounced 'conk' and also known as lambi), a rubbery mollusc served up in fritters and stews from the Florida Keys to Trinidad. As to fish, you'll find the sweet white flakes of red snapper, parrotfish and mahi-mahi (also known as dolphin, though not related to Flipper), as well as more meaty varieties such as kingfish, jackfish and tuna; and smoked marlin is a fantastic local alternative to smoked salmon.

Fresh fruits such as bananas, mangoes, pineapples and guava ripened on the tree taste twice as good as they do back home. Be sure to sample lesser known but perfectly delicious fruits such as perfumed and delicate otahite apple (also called a pommerac), golden apple (often served as a fruit juice), and the superb soursop, often made into ice creams. And no visit to Key West would be complete without a generous slice of Key Lime Pie.

Drinks

Rum, the liquor of choice in the Caribbean, is produced throughout the region, and you'll see dark, white, gold and spiced rums on offer in the shops and bars. Some are so strong, like Grenadian Jack Iron (160 per cent proof), they can even sink ice, while others, such as Jamaica's Appleton Estate 21 Year Old, are subtle sipping aged rums that you'd never dream of

Food and drink

THE BEER OF BARBADOS

Banks

Tasty local beers are brewed throughout the Caribbean

This typical Barbadian rum shop serves the national drink distilled from molasses

mixing. Rum is the basic ingredient of cocktail hour in the Caribbean. It is used in Planter's Punch (add fruit juice, a twist of lime and a dash of Angostura bitters), piña coladas (add pineapple juice and coconut cream) and iced daiquiris (whizzed up with lime juice, crushed ice and fruit syrup). Wine is imported and thus relatively expensive in the West Indies, though prices are coming down these days, so you might want to stick to cocktails or sample the local beers such as Red Stripe in Jamaica, Banks in Barbados or the ubiquitous Carib from Trinidad. International beers such as Heineken, Corona and Grolsch are also widely available, and you'll find plenty of light lagers from Europe in the French and Dutch islands. All the usual spirits,

from vodka to tequila, are available too, with well-known brands alongside slightly rougher, locally-made alternatives.

As for non-alcoholic beverages, the best choice is freshly made juices made with local fruits such as mango, golden apple, tamarind or soursop. Blended fruit punch is also refreshing and fortifying, with bananas, paw-paw, pineapple and the like blended up with ice and a dash of Grenadine, and don't miss out on trying coconut water straight from the nut. Machete-wielding vendors will chop away the husk so you can get to the water (most easily done with a straw), then chop it in half when you've finished so that you can scoop out the delicate jelly with a spoon cut from the husk.

Restaurants

The Caribbean's restaurant scene has improved in leaps and bounds over recent years, and in resort areas and capital towns you'll find a wide variety of places, serving everything from French haute cuisine to Italian, burgers, Chinese or sushi. And, of course, Caribbean cuisine is served up in top-notch, high-end restaurants as well as hole-in-the-wall eateries with a couple of tiny tables. It's not usually necessary to book ahead for lunch, though the best spots can get crowded when several ships are in town, so you might want to book ahead if you have your heart set on dining at a particular place.

Almost all tourist-oriented restaurants will have something on the menu for vegetarians, from the usual tomato pasta to stewed kidney beans with pumpkin or macaroni pie. You'll also see children's menus in the more mainstream places; where these don't exist, it's always worth asking if something special can be cooked up for the little ones.

In terms of tipping, a service charge is added to the bill in many islands; if the waiting staff have been good, you may want to add a further 10–15% on top, which is the usual range to tip in places where a service charge is not added.

Food and drink

Waterfront restaurants at Philipsburg on Dutch Sint Maarten

Entertainment

Among the most hotly discussed topics on any cruise is the standard and variety of the on-board entertainment. Most large cruise ships offer a day-long programme, which kicks off after breakfast with activities from aerobics on the pool deck to mid-morning bingo. There may be a steel band to accompany lunch, a pianist at cocktail time, and an after-dinner show. Night owls can gamble into the small hours, or disport themselves in the disco.

Obviously, the type and extent of on-board entertainment varies considerably from ship to ship. A small cruise ship cannot possibly have the facilities available to a larger vessel. It cannot, for instance, even accommodate flocks of dancing girls for Las Vegas-type show productions, let alone stage them. The passenger profile also has a bearing on the content of the entertainment programme. 'Party ships' do not offer ballroom dancing or bridge lessons; cruise lines catering for a more sedate crowd will not go in for cocktail drinking competitions or limbo dancing.

When choosing a cruise, find out what the cruise company offers in the way of entertainment. What good is a pumping disco if you like to dance in the old-fashioned way? Children may be enchanted by Disney characters at breakfast, but not the adults. Is the swimming pool big enough for you? Check whether there is a fancy dress evening, too, as you may want to pack a costume. The problem with much of the on-board entertainment is that it can appear a bit bland. But considering the cruise company's near impossible task of pleasing most of the people, perhaps this is inevitable.

Bars, lounges, and showrooms

The ship's bar (or bars) is very definitely the focus of social life on board. The main bar may feature a pianist, a cabaret act or some karaoke in the evening to accompany cocktail hour or to entertain those sitting out the main show. There is usually a pool bar for drinks on deck, too. Except on luxury 'all-inclusive' ships, drinks must be paid for in cash or charged to passengers' accounts, usually by way of a charge-card that also acts as your room key; you sign for each purchase (keep receipts), the bill will be presented at the end of the cruise. Prices are similar to those charged at a resort – not cheap.

f the bar has been declared an 'entertainment-free zone', then the evening pianist-cum-cabaret act may perform in a lounge with its own bar. During the day, lounges may be used for port talks (usually a brief history and lots of shopping information on the next port of call), bingo and trivia games or other indoor group activity. The main lounge is often referred to as the showroom or theatre. With a stage, lighting rig and theatre-style seating arrangements, this is the scene of the evening show, which can vary in content from an all-singing, all-dancing sparkly-costumed production to a variety evening featuring magicians, jugglers and comedians. This is the time when members of the cruise entertainments staff pop up to do a short turn of their own, and where passengers take to the stage if there's a talent show. There are usually two shows per evening, or the same show twice, playing for the first and second dinner seatings.

Casinos

Casinos are always closed in port due to customs regulations, but once a cruise ship sails into international waters the cards are shuffled, the slot machines jangle into life, and the serious business of on-board gambling gets underway.

It is big business for the cruise lines, and several of them operate 'cruises to nowhere', aimed specifically at gambling addicts. Many ships offer a 'full casino' with baccarat, blackjack, craps, poker and roulette, as well as the usual slot machines.

Discos and dancing

Hardly a cruise ship puts to sea without a dance floor, but facilities vary considerably. All mainstream cruise

Considering the choice of evening entertainment is crucial when choosing a cruise

ships have discos with a resident DJ who supposedly gears musical selection to the customers. Mostly this is modern dance music, but sometimes a Big Band or Swingtime evening might lure older passengers on to the dance floor. On some 'party ships' the sound system, light show and special effects are good enough to bear comparison with the best land-based nightclubs. Some ships also have a low-key club where you can just about talk over the music, or dance to a band.

Exercise facilities and spas

It is a fact that the average passenger gains around 2kg (4lb) over the duration of a week-long cruise. To redress this unhealthy situation, cruise companies usually provide a choice of exercise facilities. On a larger cruise vessel they may run the gamut from a gym and weight room or sauna and solarium to a jogging/rollerblading track, climbing wall, basketball court or bungee trampolines. The fitness director will organise aerobics or stretch classes for groups of various fitness levels and advise on other physical activities. The upper deck is generally the place to find outdoor games such as badminton, shuffleboard, table tennis and the like. On the pool deck, bathing facilities can range from the sublime (waterslides, whirlpools and surfing pools) to the faintly ridiculous (postage stamp-size pools crossed in three strokes). Almost all cruise-ship pools are filled with filtered seawater. Most mainstream

Bathing facilities can vary greatly, so make sure you check what is available on your ship

ships also have an on-board spa these days, offering everything from manicures, pedicures, facials and waxing, as well as therapeutic body treatments and all kinds of massage. Book sessions in advance, as on-board spas are often extremely popular.

Games rooms and libraries

For passengers who enjoy a gentle rubber of bridge or a nail-biting game of Risk, most ships provide a games room with card tables and a selection of board games. The library often doubles up as a venue for card players to meet, so a rowdy game of snap is probably not in order. Friendly tournaments can be arranged by the entertainments staff, and a small prize may be on offer. Shipboard libraries are not usually very extensive. There might be a modest selection of periodicals, holiday-reading type paperbacks, classics and reference books covering flora, fauna and other information about the region.

Movie theatres

A cruise can be a good way of catching up on recent-release movies. Around half-a-dozen or more films will be shown on a regular basis during a week-long cruise, usually in a designated screening room; more luxurious lines also screen movies (as well as news and other programming) on huge outdoor screens on the pool deck. Details will be listed on the daily activities programme. Most modern ships have televisions and/or DVD players in their cabins, with movies either streamed into the rooms or with satellite reception of US and other programmes, plus a DVD library.

Shore excursions

Shore excursions are supposed to be 'sightseeing made easy', taking away the hassle of arranging transport, entrance fees and a tour route yourself each time you dock, but independent-minded passengers may feel shortchanged by these all-too-brief forays. Most shore excursions depart in a convoy of coaches from the pier accompanied by a local guide, so you may feel rather like one of the herd as you and your fellow passengers pull up at the local must-see sights and completely overwhelm the place. Bear in mind also that some trips may only last for a couple of hours, so passengers wanting lunch on board can be back in time. There's plenty of choice, however, from full-day soft adventure trips involving ziplining, river rafting, horse riding or a zoom around a bobsleigh track to swimming with dolphins or hiking through the rainforest. Other tours simply package together the best of the more sedate sights. You'll be given a list of available shore excursions when you board the ship, and you can also take a look in advance on the cruise line's website – and as some trips sell out quickly, you might want to book in advance online for any trips you don't want to miss out on.

Shopping

For many cruisers, shopping in new and exotic location. rates as their most popular holiday pursuit. This will come as no surprise to the storekeepers of the Caribbean, whe welcome the souvenir-hungry tide of visiting shopaholic: with open arms. Several Caribbean cruise destinations such as St Thomas and St Martin, are duty-free port offering the promise of 25 to 50 per cent savings against US prices on some luxury goods.

On other islands, duty-free stores do a roaring trade in luxury items such as cameras, jewellery and perfumes. (Note that you often have to show your passport and ship key/charge card to make duty-free purchases.) For something with more of a local flavour, check out boutiques selling Caribbean-style fashions, or trawl the numerous galleries exhibiting local arts and crafts. Exuberant and colourful Caribbean markets are fun to explore and are a great place to pick up straw hats and mats, beach bags and fragrant packages of dried spices.

USA
Miami
With legions of shops alongside cafés and restaurants, Bayside Marketplace (*see p31*) is one of Miami's top shopping attractions. Shopping spots at Miami Beach include the Lincoln Road Mall, the galleries and antiques stores of Española Way (*see p37*), and the classy Bal Harbour mall.

Fort Lauderdale
The smart boutiques and fashionable galleries of Las Olas Boulevard are the stylish shopper's first port of call in Fort Lauderdale. For department stores head to Galleria Mall on E Sunrise Boulevard, near the beach.

Key West
Key West's main drag, Duval Street, is a magnet for shoppers. The **T-Shirt Factory** (*316 Simonton Street*) offers outlet prices and multi-purchase discounts. Just down the street, **Key West Handprint Fabrics** (*201 Simonton Street*) produces a bright range of cool cotton casualwear, plus table and furniture coverings.

Caribbean Islands
Antigua
Fresh off the ship, cruise passengers come straight into the modern **Heritage Quay** duty-free complex before reaching the streets of St John's. If you're looking for shopping with

character, head for neighbouring **Redcliffe Quay**, housed in attractively restored wooden buildings.

Aruba
A short step from the pier, **Seaport Mall** (also known as the Renaissance Mall) offers an international collection of fashion stores, jewellers and other duty-free items. For the latest in clocks and watches, Caya GF Betico Croes is the best shopping street.

Bahamas
The islands' major shopping complex, Freeport/Lucaya's **International Bazaar** and **Straw Market** on Grand Bahama Island, are pretty overwhelming to all but the most dedicated shopaholics. Store prices vary from around 20 to 40 per cent below US retail prices, while bargaining is expected in the Straw Market.

Barbados
The Bridgetown Harbour cruise ship complex and downtown Broad Street offer the widest choice of duty-free shopping in a range of boutiques and department stores. In Holetown, the attractive **Chattel House Village** offers local craft and duty-free items.

Bermuda
Tax-free Bermuda is an excellent place to stock up on life's little luxuries. The British influence is obvious in the tweeds and cashmere, the fine china and Edinburgh crystal.

Cayman Islands
Grand Cayman is a free port and British Crown Colony, so Scottish woollens, Irish linen, crystal and bone china are favourite buys. Most of the shopping action takes place on Fort Street and the Kirk Freeport Plaza.

Curaçao
Willemstad's Breedestraat, Heerenstraat, and Madurostraat are renowned for the quality and variety of their numerous stores. For lovely linen, try **New Amsterdam** (*Gomezplein 14*).

Dominica
Carib basketwork and wood sculptures are the traditional souvenirs from Dominica, available at **Kalinago Barana Autê** (*see p80*) and in the **Old Market** behind the museum on Roseau's waterfront (*see p79*).

Grenada
Don't leave Grenada without a handful of sweet-smelling spices or without browsing through the local handicrafts. In St George's, a handful of gift shops on Cross and Young streets stock attractive batik items, basketwork, jewellery and carvings; **Art Fabrick** on Young Street is a good bet, while around the corner and next to the museum, **Grenada Essentials** sell local crafts; profits go to conservation projects.

Guadeloupe
The **Centre St-John Perse** shopping complex by the cruise terminal contains

Cooking spices for sale on a market stall in Grenada

a stylish French mix of souvenir and clothing stores, perfumeries and smart little pharmacies stocking toiletries concocted from Provençal herbs. For atmosphere and spices, don't miss the noisy **Covered Market**.

Jamaica

Some of the best Jamaican souvenirs are edible or drinkable, such as Blue Mountain coffee, rum and the coffee liqueur Tia Maria. The island is also well known for its colourful tropical print fabrics transformed into attractive casualwear, and for its handicrafts.

Martinique

The jewellery stores around rue Lamartine/rue Isambert are the place to find Creole gold knot necklaces and 'slave chains' which make unusual souvenirs. Handicraft items are on sale at the **Centre des Métiers d'Art** in the Savane gardens; and Martiniquan rum is one of the best in the Caribbean.

Puerto Rico

Calle Fortaleza and Calle San Francisco form two seamless stretches of T-shirt and jewellery stores, fashion boutiques, craft shops and galleries. The **Centro de Artes Populares**, in the Convento de los Domínicos, Plaza de San José, offers a full range of Puerto Rican crafts.

St Barthélemy

As befits a duty-free port, Gustavia's shops carry a good selection of luxury items, but bargains are few and far between. The only local handicraft of note is basketweaving. In addition to sunhats, bread baskets are a speciality.

St Croix

The best shopping is in Christiansted, around Strandgade and Kongensgade. **Folk Art Traders**, on Strandgade, stocks a wealth of colourful Caribbean crafts and more unusual items such as jewellery made from larimar (a semi-precious sky-blue stone), genuine 'pieces of eight' (old Spanish coins) and Haitian paintings. Another favourite is St Croix's own high-quality Cruzan rum.

St Kitts

Gifts, clothing and duty-free items are all available from the waterfront **Pelican Mall** complex, while near the Circus, **All Kind of Tings** on Liverpool Row holds several stalls selling local crafts.

St Lucia

The attractive new **Pointe Seraphine** duty-free complex right by the cruise-ship pier offers one-stop shopping for everything from a little black frock to a helicopter tour of the island. Check out the **Craft Market** on the waterfront.

St Martin/Sint Maarten

On the French side of the island, Marigot has its fair share of chic boutiques and Gallic goodies, as well as a mix of shopping and dining at the **Marina Royale** complex. Front Street, Philipsburg, is a duty-free shopping haven with great deals on all sorts of luxury items such as jewellery, watches and leather, while the Philipsburg Market Place on Back Street has a wide selection of local crafts.

St Thomas

Shopping in downtown Charlotte Amalie is not for the faint-hearted. Over 400 shops are crammed into the area between Main Street and the waterfront, and they are packed with

Traditional costumed dolls dressed in bright Madras cotton on sale in Guadeloupe

every conceivable luxury and souvenir item. For shopping at a less frenetic pace, **Tillet Gardens**, near Tutu, is a delightful artisans' enclave.

St Vincent and the Grenadines

Shopping is a very low-key affair in Kingstown. The **St Vincent Craftsman's Centre** on Frenches Street is the main craft market, and well worth a browse. Bequia offers more choice with a selection of beach-style boutiques selling silkscreen pareos (brightly coloured cotton wraparounds) and swimwear. Along the waterfront in Port Elizabeth, local craftspeople sell handmade model boats; the best ones are available from the **Seargeant and Mauvin** workshops on the northwest side of the harbour.

Tortola

Road Town's shops are in cosy wooden houses on Main Street, and include the foodie temptations of **Sunny Caribbee** (guava jelly, spicy chutneys and wooden pots of West Indian Hangover Cure), and **Pussers** (yachting clothing, scrimshaw carving, rum and other nautical stuff).

Trinidad and Tobago

Frederick Street, in Port of Spain, is one huge international bazaar with everything from Swiss watches and Swedish silver to Indian saris and calypso CDs. Craft stores also abound at Pigeon Point and Store Bay beaches on Tobago.

Sport and leisure

Watersports, quite obviously, are the name of the game in the Caribbean. But, there is plenty for landlubbers too: fishing, hiking, golf, cycling, tennis and horse-riding are on offer throughout the islands. Local tourist offices and their overseas branches have details of most sports facilities and special sporting events.

Cycling

At weekends, the French islands of Martinique and Guadeloupe are a blur of lycra-clad cyclists tearing up and down swooping mountain roads. Mountain bikes (called VTT in French, pronounced 'vay-tay-tay') can be hired for the day or by the hour on many islands; Bermuda's Railway Trail (*see p68*) is especially good for cycling.

Diving and snorkelling

Some specialist cruise vessels, such as the Windstar ships, are fully equipped with scuba and snorkelling gear, while others offer snorkelling as a shore excursion option. Experienced (certificated) divers will have no problem finding dive operators offering trips on all the Caribbean islands. Snorkellers can paddle about off any beach to their heart's content. You can hire fins and masks from dive shops or watersports outlets on many Caribbean beaches; many places offer guided snorkelling trips.

The best dive sites in the Caribbean are found off the Bahamas, Grand Cayman and the Dutch Leeward Islands.

Golf

Golf is an increasingly popular pastime in the Caribbean, and there are courses springing up all over the place, many of them designed by international names such as Robert Trent Jones and numbering among the most challenging and beautiful in the world – picture fairways with a backdrop of the glistening Caribbean sea, the odd waterfall, and shade, courtesy of palm trees. Many are attached to resort complexes, but even these welcome visitors, and can arrange equipment hire, instruction and caddies. Note that carts and caddies are mandatory at some Caribbean courses.

During the busy winter season, it is advisable to make arrangements to play in advance, but even a last-minute enquiry may be successful as cruise ship timing often means playing during the hottest part of the day.

Grand Bahama has some of the best courses in the Caribbean, as does Jamaica and Bermuda. For sheer scenery, it would be hard to beat Mahogany Run in St Thomas.

Florida is a golfer's paradise. There are dozens of courses in the Greater Miami and Greater Fort Lauderdale areas. Contact the relevant Visitors and Convention Bureau, which should be able to provide you with a golfing guide.

Hiking and walking

Ecotourism is a growth industry in the islands as an increasing number of visitors quit the beaches in search of the 'real Caribbean'. Rainforest trails, mountain lakes and volcanic craters provide a wealth of stupendous scenery and a great opportunity to stretch your legs – and many islands have lovely interior waterfalls in which to take a dip, too. Local guiding companies have sprung up all over the place, and their services are recommended for anybody keen to step off the beaten track. Without a knowledgeable local expert, it is easy to get lost. Paths and trails can disappear with alarming speed, washed away by floods or simply reclaimed by the undergrowth. Day-long hikes are often impractical for cruise passengers, as they tend to start at dawn, the coolest time of day, long before the cruise ships have lowered their gangplanks. But it is still possible to get away from it all on shorter trails and in the many national parks. Tourist offices can provide lists of guides (you may like to contact them in advance), and often carry information and maps covering short island walks or historic walks around town. We've also pointed to some of the more accessible trails in this book's destination guide. Always dress comfortably for hiking – sturdy shoes and loose-fitting cotton clothes are recommended, while long trousers will protect your legs from scratches

The Caribbean Islands and Florida Keys offer some of the finest diving in the world

and insect bites. Always take a hat and plenty of water, and bear in mind that walking in the rainforest means that showers are likely, so you might want to bring along a light, waterproof coat.

Horse riding

This is a great way to explore off the beaten track. Local tourist offices will have a list of riding stables offering guided treks in the countryside, with guides pointing out local sights and fauna and flora, while beach rides are increasingly popular – in many islands, you can even swim on your horse in the sea, a truly memorable experience. Most stables can supply hard hats, but it's a good idea to wear long trousers to prevent your legs chafing against the saddle. If beach riding is on the menu, the stables will provide a place for you to change in and out of swimming gear, and transport your belongings back to and from the departure point to the beach.

Sport fishing

Most Caribbean marinas harbour a sport-fishing operator or two. There is no mistaking those elevated lookout towers and the selection of whippy-looking rods lined up on stern designed to lure passing anglers aboard. Deep-sea fishing for wahoo, tuna, marlin, mahi-mahi (also known as 'dolphin' – not to be confused with the friendly mammal of the same name) and the magnificent sailfish is available off most of the islands. One of the

hottest spots for the fishing fraternity is Grand Cayman, which also reckons to have the best bonefishing in the world, and devotes the month of June to the Million Dollar Month Fishing Tournament. There are deep-sea fishing charter operators offering full- and half-day charters, all equipment supplied, on almost all of the islands; tourist offices can supply listings. Florida is also a big-time sport-fishing centre. Fort Lauderdale's Bahia Mar Yachting Center is chock-full of gleaming charter fishing boats; you could also head north to Pompano Beach (11km/7 miles), the modestly-titled Swordfish Capital of the World,

The Florida Keys are a magnet for keen anglers. Every marina has its sport-fishing charter boats, and barely a month goes by without a big-money fishing tournament run out of Islamorada in the Middle Keys.

Tennis

It is not usually easy for cruise ship passengers to find a tennis court, as most of them are attached to hotels and reserved for the use of guests. However, check with the local tourist office for news of friendly resorts or rare public courts. Smarter hotels may insist on players wearing whites on court.

Watersports

As a rule of thumb, wherever there are beachfront hotels there are bound to be watersports facilities, with watersports

Big blue: windsurfing off the Bahamas

outfits run either by the hotels or independent operators. In major resort areas, waterskiing, jet skiing and parasailing are all part of the fun. Windsurfers, pedalboats, Hobie Cats, Sunfish and other small sailing boats are also widely available for rental, and more adventurous possibilities include kitesurfing, a cross between windsurfing and regular surfing, wherever the trade winds blow strongly enough. Another favourite pursuit is a coastal cruise on board a catamaran, which allows you a close-up view of each island's coastal scenery, as well as the chance to stop for a bit of snorkelling over the best of the reefs (boats carry masks and fins). Most cruise lines offer sailing or catamaran trips as a shore excursion option; lunch and unlimited drinks are usually included in the price.

Soft adventure

As a means of offering something different to visitors (and with an eye firmly on cruise-shippers saturated by endless beaches and forts), companies in several islands across the region offer various adrenaline-fuelled activities, from swinging through the treetops attached to a zipline to tubing along tumbling rivers or speeding along a bobsleigh track. You can also swing high above the rainforest in a gondola, have a ride on a dog-pulled sleigh, speed around on an ATV bike, explore the sea bed with breathing apparatus courtesy of a spaceman-like fishbowl helmet or from the comfort of a submarine. All of these attractions are geared toward cruisers, and tend to be among the more popular of the shore excursions offered on ships, so it's a good idea to book early.

Children

Once upon a time, a child on a cruise ship was the proverbial lonely little petunia in an onion patch. The odd nanny-supervised tea party and a three-legged race around the deck was considered 'entertainment', and the rest of the time a child's role was to be rarely seen and absolutely never heard. Now, all that has changed, and junior cruisers have never had it so good.

In recent years, cruise companies have grabbed a significant slice of the family holiday market by offering a raft of tempting fare deals, special facilities and the promise of a safe and easily supervised environment. Most ships provide some form of organised children's programme, while others are exclusively family-orientated, offering state of the art facilities that will blow most children away. Most will also have kids' clubs catering for different age groups. When booking a family cruise holiday, it is important to find out not only what the cruise company offers in the way of activities, but also what age group these are aimed at.

Activity programmes

These can vary tremendously in content and in the frequency with which they are offered. Some ships only run children's programmes on days when the ship is at sea, or during the school holidays. Child-orientated lines such as the Disney Cruise Line offer a full daily programme of events for children and teenagers of all ages year-round, and all Caribbean cruises make stops at Disney's Castaway Cay, a private island in the Bahamas dedicated to entertaining children – from facility-packed beaches to the Flying Dutchman ghost ship that appeared in the Pirates of the Caribbean movies. Activity programmes can incorporate anything from dressing up as pirates for a pool party to playing computer games on a giant-screen Nintendo Wii or on-deck

SUN ALERT

Everybody has to take care in the hot Caribbean sun, but children are particularly susceptible to its burning rays. Make sure they are well covered with a high-factor sun cream every morning before going out to play. Top it up during the day, and dress them in UV-filter swimwear that covers their arms and shoulders; hats with a peak, and a flap to protect the neck are also essential. It's also sensible to keep them out of the sun in the middle of the day, when the rays are at their strongest.

ice-skating. Arts and crafts classes, quizzes and magic shows may also be on offer. Most cruise lines provide a supervised children's play area, and there may be swimming and sports instruction or a water-park or 'Flow-rider' surfing pool, too. Some of the best and most broad-ranging children's programmes are offered by Royal Caribbean, Carnival Cruise Line, Celebrity Cruises and Norwegian Cruise Line.

Babies

There is no reason baby should not come too, but parents would be advised to make a few enquiries first, as some cruise lines will not allow passengers under the age of two. With adequate advance warning (at the time of booking), cruise lines will provide cots, high chairs and other baby and toddler paraphernalia. Check if baby food and formula are available on board. Again, advance warning will do the trick, but

nappies are generally not part of the service. Parents travelling with small children, or those who fancy dinner without the kids every now and then, should check the availability of baby-sitters in advance. Some ships provide a pool of child-minders for both day and night duty, either for free or for a small hourly rate. On non-child-orientated vessels, parents may have to make arrangements with a sympathetic staff member, or other parents.

Kids' cuisine

Parents of fussy eaters would do well to check out children's catering arrangements ahead of time. Most children would trade all the gourmet delicacies in the world for a fish finger or a hamburger and fries, and the more child-friendly cruise lines recognise this by providing special children's menus. As a rule, families with young children will be given the early dinner sitting (around 6.30pm or 7pm).

On-board pools will provide hours of fun

Cruising and cruise ships

Gone are the days when the average cruise passenger was as old as the hills and as rich as Croesus. Today's cruisers come from all walks of life and every age range. Their interests are diverse and their expectations high.

Cruise lines have risen to the challenge in style. In order to keep up with the passenger boom and the demand for higher standards and better facilities, they are introducing new cruise vessels at staggering rates. Never before has the potential passenger been confronted with such a wide choice.

Cruise ships can be roughly divided into four main categories: deluxe, luxury, premium and standard. Somewhere between the top-of-the-range deluxe cruise vessels, with an atmosphere similar to that of an exclusive private yacht, and the monster party ships plying the Bahamas route, there is something to suit everyone.

Categories

Deluxe

Small and perfectly formed, the deluxe cruise ship is effectively a floating luxury boutique hotel with a capacity of 50 to 200 passengers. Its hallmarks are gourmet cuisine, exemplary service and a high staff/passenger ratio. Key

deluxe lines offering Caribbean cruises are Seabourn and SeaDream.

Luxury

Luxury-class vessels attract a sophisticated and high-spending crowd. They provide elegantly appointed and large cabins, all of which will be sea-facing, and some of which will have private verandas. Standards of cuisine are extremely high and guests dress for dinner. Facilities vary with the size of the ship (from around 900 to 2500), but generally organised on-board events are infrequent. The emphasis is on informal relaxation. Notable in this category are the Cunard, Silversea, Regent Seven Seas and Crystal lines.

Premium

The majority of mainstream cruise vessels fall into the premium class. They are owned by experienced cruise companies, maintained and run to a high standard, and offer an enjoyable cruising holiday with good food and a broad range of entertainment. Guests will have the opportunity to dress up for a couple of formal nights. At the top end of this category are Celebrity Cruises, Holland America, Princess Cruise Lines and Royal Caribbean.

Sail-cruise vessels

For a cruise experience with a difference, there are several sail-cruise ships plying Caribbean waters, carrying between 150 and 270 passengers.

Standard

Standard cruise vessels are aimed at a more casual crowd. It is difficult to type-cast them as they cover a broad spectrum from the huge modern party ships to older vessels with fewer modern facilities.

Deluxe lines
Seabourn and SeaDream

Styled as luxury yachts with a capacity of 208 passengers (Seabourn) and 112 (SeaDream), these elegant, upscale vessels offer cruising for the seriously rich; think complimentary on-deck massages and iced champagne served to you in the whirlpool. The entertainment is suitably refined too.
Seabourn. Tel: 1-800/929 9391 (US);
0845 070 0500 (UK);
www.seabourn.com
SeaDream. Tel: (305) 631 6100 (in US);
0800 783 1373 (UK);
www.seadreamyachtclub.com

Luxury lines
Crystal

With a capacity of around 1000 passengers, Crystal's spacious, upmarket ships are known for their excellent service and cuisine combined with the increased facilities that their size allows. You'll find large, well-equipped spas, fitness centres, putting greens, and, of course, pools. Enrichment is excellent, with informed lectures and hands-on classes in such things as gourmet cooking or bridge, while entertainment consists of classy shows, tinkling pianos and films in the movie theatre.
Tel: 1-866/446 6625 (US);
0207 287 9040 (UK);
www.crystalcruises.com.

Cunard

Cunard is one of the oldest upper-end companies, with the huge *Queen Mary II* having replaced the now retired *QE2*, and another luxurious behemoth, the *Queen Elizabeth*, due to set sail in 2010. Some of the grandest ocean liners ever built, Cunard's ships hold between 2,000 and 3,000 passengers, and facilities are excellent. There's a real British flavour to the daily afternoon tea service, and good facilities for families, ranging from 'nannies' for the little ones to structured activities for young teens.
Tel 1-800/728 6273 (US);
www.cunard.com
0845/071 0300 (UK);
www.cunard.co.uk

A cruise ship docked on the island of St Thomas

Regent Seven Seas

Elegant, comfortable ships with the emphasis on personal service and an 'upscale but not uptight' attitude. Passenger capacity ranges from 330 to 700, so they never feel too crowded, and between 70 and 90% of cabins have their own private balconies, one of the highest percentages in the industry.
Tel: (877) 505 5370 (US);
02380 682 280 (UK); www.rssc.com

Silversea

With one foot in the deluxe category, Silversea ships carry between 300 and 540 guests, and offer a truly premium experience, from crystal glasses on the dinner tables to a fully all-inclusive policy for gourmet food and top-quality wines and spirits. The enrichment programmes are more varied and detailed than their competitors, and there's the obligatory pool, movie theatre, casino, spa, and fitness centre, too.
Tel: 1-800/722 9955 (US);
0844 770 9040 (UK);
www.silversea.com

Premium lines

Carnival

The originator of the 'Fun Ship' and still delivering today, with a fleet of colourful, amenity-packed ships decorated in a riot of bright colours – subtle, they're not. The 22 megaships in their fleet are huge, with spacious cabins and passenger capacity of anything between 1500 and 3600. From climbing walls to surf pools, the amenities are endless, as are the dining and partying options. Good facilities both for children and adults, with designated kid-free zones.
Tel: (305) 406 4779 (US); 0845 351 0556 (UK); www.carnival.com

Celebrity

One of the more upscale of the mainstream lines; ships are bedecked in expensive original artwork, but there's none of the stuffiness of the deluxe fleets. Nonetheless, they're elegant and stylish, with a passenger capacity of between 1000 and 3000. Facilities include spas, casinos, variety shows, basketball courts and gyms, and there are pretty good enrichment programmes, too.
Tel: 1-800/647 2251 (US); 0845 456 1520 (UK); www.celebritycruises.com

Norwegian

One of the older cruise lines, and one of the first to cruise the Caribbean, Norwegian's fleet is anything but old, with many of the ships spanking new with colourful exterior paintwork.

Ships have a casual feel, with a 'Freestyle Cruising' policy that means lots of choices when it comes to dining options, and plenty of sporting amenities.
Tel: 1-866/625 1166 (US); 0845 201 8912 (UK); www.ncl.com

P&O

Britain's premier cruise line, with a fleet of seven ships decorated with original British artworks, and restaurants created by celebrity chefs Gary Rhodes and Marco Pierre White. Facilities include pools, spas, bungee trampolines and, on the Ventura family ship, a circus skills training centre; family ships also have various kids' clubs organized by age.
Tel: 0845 678 0014 (UK); www.pocruises.com

Princess

This extensive mainstream fleet has ships which range in passenger capacity from 1000 to 3000, with some targeted toward families, and others with more adult-oriented facilities. All, however, have 'Personal Choice Cruising', which gives you plenty of choice in terms of dining options, cabin class and the like.
Tel: (661) 753 0000 (US); 0845 373 5922 (UK); www.princess.com

Royal Caribbean

A mega-ship fleet which makes much of its extensive amenities, from ice rinks, climbing walls, PADI scuba certification and golf simulators to multiple restaurants and bars. In terms of entertainment, there are bingo nights, variety shows, and discos, while kids and teens are well catered for with organised programmes.
Tel: (800) 398 9819 (US); 0844 493 4005 (UK); www.royalcaribbean.com

Sailing lines
Star Clippers

Full-blown sailing ships with capacity for just 170 to 220 passengers, Star Clippers are intimate ships, with the usual spas and pools as well as marina decks from which to swim or indulge in watersports, and quirky touches such as underwater portholes. Guests are able to help sail the vessels, and even climb the masts.
Tel: (305) 442 0550 (US); 01473 292 029 (UK); www.starclippers.com

Windstar

Luxury is the name of the game here, with cabins equipped with everything from Bose sound systems and iPod Nanos to L'Occitane soaps and fluffy robes; on deck, meanwhile, the sails unfurl at the touch of a button. Passenger capacity of 148 or 312, so things never feel crowded, and there's a watersports platform for swimming, snorkelling and the like.
Tel: (206) 281 3535 (US); 0207 292 2387 (UK);
www.windstarcruises.com

Essentials

Arriving

British visitors and other nationals from countries participating in the USA Visa Waiver programme simply require a valid passport and completed waiver form (supplied) to enter the USA or the US Virgin Islands. Make sure that the form gives the full address of your first night's accommodation.

For many years, American and Canadian visitors did not require passports to visit any Caribbean country, but these days, all travellers re-entering the USA must present a passport on re-entry to the United States. US citizens can use a US passport card instead of a full passport if their Caribbean cruise begins and ends in the same port; for more details on how to obtain one of these, see the International Travel pages of the US Department of State website (*travel.state.gov*) Visas are seldom necessary for nationals of the European Union visiting the Caribbean islands – a valid passport will suffice. Your passport may be held by the crew after boarding for the duration of the cruise so that staff can clear entry to the islands on your behalf, thus saving you lots of time and hassle. Your documents will be returned once the ship has departed its last port of call and is en route back to the home port.

Cruise passengers commencing or ending their cruise in a Caribbean country will be required to fill out an immigration form. These are handed out on board aircraft or the cruise ship. Immigration rules are strictly enforced throughout the region, and the immigration authorities will need to see an onward ticket. The accommodation section of the immigration form must be completed, or entry may be refused.

Ground transport

Where possible, arrange airport transfers through the cruise company. Those arriving at Miami, Fort Lauderdale and Puerto Rico's San Juan airports will find taxis readily available. Most Caribbean airports have tourist information desks which advise on ground transport and taxi fares. The journey from Miami airport to the Port of Miami takes around 30 minutes; from Fort Lauderdale airport to Port Everglades takes ten minutes; from San Juan's Luis Muñoz Marín airport to the Old Town cruise piers is 45 minutes. At Miami and Fort Lauderdale airports, SuperShuttle (*see p30*) minibuses offer a quick and inexpensive door-to-door alternative to taxis.

Climate

The Caribbean Sea and its semicircle of islands lie in the tropics, so year-round temperatures remain high with little variation. Though temperatures can top 38°C (100°F), this is a rare occurrence, and the heat is generally tempered by cooling trade winds. Daytime temperatures in the Caribbean average between 26 and 30°C (79 and 86°F); night-time temperatures are around 15–18°C (59–64°F).

The coolest and driest months are at the height of the December to April season. May/June and October/November are wet, though tropical showers (particularly in rainforest areas) can occur year-round. 'Hurricanes hardly happen', but if they do, they usually choose September or October.

Conversion tables
See p173.

T-shirts are always in US sizes. Florida, the US Virgin Islands, Puerto Rico, and other US-influenced islands follow the US system of sizes; Commonwealth islands follow the UK system; French and Dutch-influenced communities use the Rest of Europe sizes.

Crime
Violent crime is rare on the smaller Caribbean islands, but on larger and busier islands, such as Jamaica,

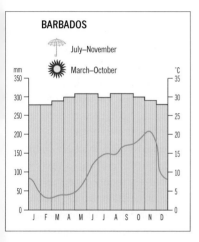

BARBADOS

July–November

March–October

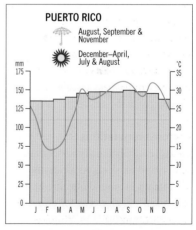

PUERTO RICO

August, September & November

December–April, July & August

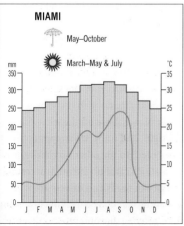

MIAMI

May–October

March–May & July

WEATHER CONVERSION CHART

25.4mm = 1 inch

°F = 1.8 × °C + 32

Trinidad or St Thomas, it is unwise to walk down unlit streets or along the beach after dark. Petty theft is a problem. Do not leave watches, wallets and cameras unattended on the beach. Carry cash in a money belt or tamper-proof waist pack.

Violent crime in Florida has been making the headlines for several years, though, to a large extent, the danger is limited to a handful of non-tourist trouble spots such as the Liberty City and Overtown districts of Miami. However, basic rules of the jungle in any city advise you to leave any valuables in your hotel, carry only small amounts of cash and always stick to busy, well-lit streets after dark. If in doubt, do not walk; instead, take a taxi. Rental car companies in Florida hand out a list of simple safety precautions that should be observed. In the event of an accident, find a well-lit telephone – gas stations, stores, or restaurants are recommended – and dial *911*. This call is free, even from pay phones, and connects with the emergency services.

Customs regulations

Alcohol and tobacco allowances vary from island to island. As a rule, the limit stands at around one litre of spirits and 200 cigarettes for every adult (over 18), as in the USA. Visitors from the USA can re-enter the States with up to US$800-worth of duty-free goods, or US$1,600 if returning from the US Virgin Islands. British visitors have an allowance of £340 on return to the UK.

Foreign travellers departing from the USA within 48 hours are exempt from USA customs duties. It is important to remember that black coral and turtle products cannot be imported into Australia, the USA, the UK and many other countries.

Departure tax

Most Caribbean islands levy a departure tax on visitors. Cruise passengers do not pay this unless they are flying home from one of the islands. The actual amount varies from island to island, though in the Eastern Caribbean, it is around EC$50. US dollars are usually accepted.

Driving and car rental

Car rental is readily available on most islands, but few cruise passengers with a limited stay choose to take up the option. In addition to a full national or international driver's licence several Caribbean islands also require drivers to purchase a temporary local licence (usually available from the rental car company), which adds to the cost. Check the type of insurance the rental company provides very carefully. Often the driver is liable for the first US$1,000 of any damage done to the vehicle. Some islands drive on the left, some on the right, and some are swapping from one system to the other, so check regulations carefully before you travel. Caribbean roads and drivers are 'adventurous'. Maybe too adventurous for a relaxing day out!

Car rental in Florida is inexpensive and easy. All the major car rental agencies have concessions throughout the state. Fly-drive deals can offer excellent value for money, and petrol (gas) is cheap. Driving is on the right. The top speed limit on the highway is 88km (55mph); on some sections of interstate roads this is raised to 105km (65mph).

Electricity

The electrical current in the USA and US Virgin Islands is 110 volts AC. Most other Caribbean islands have a 220 volt electricity supply. Cruise passengers with electrical equipment such as shavers and hairdryers should check with the cruise line as to what adaptors are necessary.

Emergencies

In the USA, the police and emergency services can be summoned by a free call to *911*. In the Caribbean islands, the numbers vary and may be anything from three (usually *911* or *999*) to seven digits long. Free brochures from the local tourist office usually list all the useful numbers on the island. Pick one up before leaving the main town.

Etiquette

Dress is invariably casual in the Caribbean and in Florida. Few restaurants require men to wear a jacket, especially at lunchtime when most cruisers visit, and ties are almost

CONVERSION TABLE

FROM	TO	MULTIPLY BY
Inches	Centimetres	2.54
Feet	Metres	0.3048
Yards	Metres	0.9144
Miles	Kilometres	1.6090
Acres	Hectares	0.4047
Gallons	Litres	4.5460
Ounces	Grams	28.35
Pounds	Grams	453.6
Pounds	Kilograms	0.4536
Tons	Tonnes	1.0160

To convert back, for example from centimetres to inches, divide by the number in the third column.

MEN'S SUITS

UK	36	38	40	42	44	46	48
Rest of Europe	46	48	50	52	54	56	58
USA	36	38	40	42	44	46	48

DRESS SIZES

UK	8	10	12	14	16	18
France	36	38	40	42	44	46
Italy	38	40	42	44	46	48
Rest of Europe	34	36	38	40	42	44
USA	6	8	10	12	14	16

MEN'S SHIRTS

UK	14	14.5	15	15.5	16	16.5	17
Rest of Europe	36	37	38	39/40	41	42	43
USA	14	14.5	15	15.5	16	16.5	17

MEN'S SHOES

UK	7	7.5	8.5	9.5	10.5	11
Rest of Europe	41	42	43	44	45	46
USA	8	8.5	9.5	10.5	11.5	12

WOMEN'S SHOES

UK	4.5	5	5.5	6	6.5	7
Rest of Europe	38	38	39	39	40	41
USA	6	6.5	7	7.5	8	8.5

Blooming marvellous: brilliant Caribbean flora attracts the birds and butterflies

extinct – though in the Caribbean save beachwear for the beach. Wearing swimsuits when shopping, for example, can cause offence.

Topless bathing is forbidden in Florida, and on all but the French Caribbean islands. However, it is unofficially sanctioned on certain sections of many Caribbean beaches presided over by resort hotels. If you want to get an all-over tan, ask hotel staff before stripping off.

Health

No inoculations or vaccinations are required for visits to the Caribbean or Florida. Tap water is drinkable in most Caribbean countries, but it's best to stick to bottled water. Ice is usually made from boiled or purified water.

Do not let sunburn ruin your holiday. Be sure to use a high-factor suncream and keep visits to the beach or pool deck short for the first few days.

Mosquitoes can be a real problem for visitors to Florida's Everglades and certainly in most Caribbean islands, particularly in the summer season. Wise travellers carry a plentiful supply of repellent. Another potential health hazard is the machineel tree. Tall, bushy, and fond of a beachfront situation, the machineel has highly poisonous apple-like fruit and milky sap that can cause painful blisters and swelling if it comes into contact with skin. Do not even take shelter under these trees in a downpour, as the runoff is dangerous.

All cruise ships have a doctor and some have infirmaries equipped to cope with emergencies. Passengers taking strong medication, or with a condition that might require treatment during the cruise, should inform the cruise line in advance and renotify the ship's doctor soon after embarking.

Media

Most cruise ships have satellite access to American cable news. American periodicals are sold around the Caribbean. Internet access is available on almost all ships, but is cheaper at

Look for shade at midday

the Internet cafés that you'll find at the majority of cruise-ship terminals, or in an island's capital town.

Money matters

The US dollar is local currency in Puerto Rico, the US Virgin Islands and the British Virgin Islands. The common currency in the Eastern Caribbean is the Eastern Caribbean dollar (EC$) which has a fixed rate of exchange against the US dollar, as has the Bermuda dollar (BD$). The Bahamanian dollar (BS$) is kept on par with the US dollar, while the Jamaican dollar (JM$) and the Trinidad and Tobago dollar (TT$) fluctuate. French islands use the euro. The American dollar is accepted throughout the islands, although change will probably be given in local currency.

Credit cards and traveller's cheques are used widely to free tourists from the hazards of carrying large amounts of cash. Although some countries accept other denominations, Thomas Cook recommend US dollar cheques. These can frequently be used to settle bills in larger restaurants and tourist shops without the need to cash them first.

Sustainable tourism

Thomas Cook is a strong advocate of ethical and fairly traded tourism and believes that the travel experience should be as good for the places visited as it is for the people who visit them. That's why we firmly support The Travel Foundation, a charity that develops solutions to help improve and protect holiday destinations, their environment, traditions and culture. To find out what you can do to make a positive difference to the places you travel to and the people who live there, please visit *www.thetravelfoundation.org.uk*

Telephones

The Caribbean telephone system is generally efficient and easy to use. There are plenty of public telephones that operate with coins and telephone cards. Cards are recommended for making direct dial international calls. They can be bought from post offices, many shops, and information offices. Calls made on board ships can be very expensive – it's far better to wait until you disembark on the islands. Several of the mainstream cruise companies have facilities for passengers to use their own mobile phones when on board (the ship carries its own transmitter); you'll pay the usual high international roaming charges. In the USA 'calling cards', readily purchased, may be used for long-distance calls. Avoid making long-distance calls from your hotel room to avoid surcharges levied by the hotel.

Country codes

Australia *61*	**France** *33*
Germany *49*	**Ireland** *353*
Netherlands *31*	**Spain** *34*
UK *44*	**US** *1*

Time

Eastern Florida, the Bahamas and Jamaica observe Eastern Standard Time (GMT minus five hours). Bermuda and the rest of the Caribbean countries are an hour ahead (GMT minus four hours).

Tipping

Tipping is one of the 'hidden extras' most cruise passengers have to face. Some luxury cruise ships have abolished it, while some have an automatic gratuity policy in which a service charge is added to your account – essentially on most cruise vessels, tips comprise an important slice of the staff's income, and will add up to between US$10 and $15 per passenger per day. It is customary to tip the dining room staff and cabin steward on the last night on board. Most cruise lines provide tipping guidelines, perhaps included in a disembarkation talk on the last day of the cruise, or in a printed list on their website or in documentation given to you; a list may also be left in your cabin along with envelopes marked with the name of the various recipients. As a basic guide, expect to tip the regular waiter and cabin steward US$3.50, and the busboy US$2.00, per passenger per day; the maître d'hôtel US$10 for the whole trip; and the wine steward 15 per cent of the wine bill. All tips should be given in cash (preferably US dollars). Bar stewards can be tipped during the cruise.

On land, the attitude to tipping is fairly aggressive in both Florida and the Caribbean. Taxi drivers expect 10 to 15 per cent; the same for restaurant bills if service is not included. Tip bellhops around US$1/EC$2.50 per item.

Tourist information

In many cruise ports, there is a tourist office or tourist information point located on the pier. Staff will be able to provide maps, taxi fare guidelines and assistance with general enquiries about car rental, shopping, sports facilities, walking tours and hiking guides. For holiday-makers who would like additional information or accommodation lists before departure, many Caribbean countries have overseas offices in the USA and the UK, as well as head offices which you will find listed throughout this guide.

Travellers with disabilities

Many cruise lines are wary of travellers with disabilities and their attitude can be far from encouraging; however, most lines have modified a few cabins to provide a wheelchair-friendly layout – the newer the ship, the better the facilities. It is important to make enquiries well in advance of the proposed travel date. Contact a cruise agency such as www.cruisingholiday.co.uk who specialise in advising on cruise holidays for travellers with mobility problems.

Directory

Accommodation price guide

All price ranges given are for a double room exclusive of taxes.

★	Under $100
★★	$100–150
★★★	over $150

Eating out price guide

The star rating indicates the approximate cost per person per meal, not including alcohol.

★	under US$20
★★	between US$20–40
★★★	over US$40

MIAMI

ACCOMMODATION

Hotel Astor ★

Art deco boutique hotel in the heart of South Beach with smart, modern rooms and a good restaurant.
956 Washington Avenue, South Beach.
Tel: (305) 531 8081;
www.hotelastor.com

Conrad Miami ★★

Stylish place with great views of Biscayne Bay; conveniently located for downtown Miami's shopping and restaurants.
1395 Brickell Avenue, Miami.
Tel: (305) 503 6500;
www.conradmiami.com

EATING AND DRINKING

Joe's Stone Crab Restaurant ★★

A seafood institution, with 'early Miami-Beach décor'.

11 Washington Ave, South Miami Beach.
Tel: (305) 673 0365.
Open: mid-Oct–mid-May daily 11.30am–2pm; mid-May–mid-Oct Sun 4–10pm, Mon–Thur 5–10pm, Fri & Sat 5–11pm.

Versailles ★★/★★★

Spacious Little Havana landmark serving excellent Cuban cuisine.
3555 SW 8th St, Little Havana.
Tel: (305) 444 0420.
Open: Mon–Thur 8am–2am; Fri 8am–3am; Sat 8am–4:30am; Sun 9am–1am.

Nemo ★★★

Busy, buzzing place offering a delicious fusion of tastes from the Caribbean to the Middle East; great Sunday brunch, too.
100 Collins Ave, Miami Beach.
Tel: (305) 532 4550.

Open: Mon–Sat noon–3pm & 6.30–midnight, Sun 11am–3pm & 6.30pm–midnight.

ENTERTAINMENT

Fillmore Miami Beach at The Jackie Gleason Theater

Gorgeous Art Deco theatre staging a wide range of plays, dance performances, comedy and even the occasional boxing match.
1700 Washington Avenue, South Beach.
Tel: (305) 673 7300;
www.fillmoremb.com

Tobacco Road

Miami's oldest bar. Daily dinner specials, from all-you-can-eat barbecue to lobster dinners, plus regular live music.
626 South Miami Ave.
Tel: (305) 374 1198;
www.tobacco-road.com.
Open: daily 10am–late.

Van Dyke Café
The upstairs lounge of this grill restaurant has live jazz, blues and Brazilian music every evening.
Lincoln Road Mall, 846 Lincoln Road, Miami Beach. Tel: (305) 534 3600. Open: daily 10am–1am.

SPORTS AND LEISURE
Fiesta Cruises
Sightseeing tours around Biscayne Bay aboard a catamaran.
Slip 6, Miamarina, Bayside Marketplace, 401 Biscayne Blvd. Tel: (305) 371 3033.

Thriller Miami
Powerboat tours in Biscayne Bay from the Bayside Marketplace – an adrenaline-filled way to see the city and environs including the so-called Millionaire's Row – from the sea.
Bayside Marketplace, 401 Biscayne Blvd. Tel: (305) 373 7001; www.thrillermiami.com

FORT LAUDERDALE
ACCOMMODATION
The Pillars at New River Sound ★★★
Appealing boutique hotel with lovely décor and a great waterfront location overlooking the Intracoastal Waterway.
111 North Birch Road. Tel: (954) 763 2845; www.pillarshotel.com

Riverside Hotel ★★★
Lovely old hotel first opened in the 1930s with handsome modern rooms, a pool and a restaurant and bar.
620 East Las Olas Blvd. Tel: (954) 467 0671; www.riversidehotel.com

EATING AND DRINKING
The Cheesecake Factory ★★
Something for everyone, from eggs and appetisers to pastas and seafoods. And, of course, the cheesecake desserts – you can indulge in more than 20 varieties.
2612 Sawgrass Mills Circle. Tel: (954) 835 0966. Open: Mon–Thur 11am–11.30pm, Fri & Sat 11.30am–12.30am, Sun 10am–11pm.

15th St Fisheries ★★★
Award-winning Florida seafood restaurant on the Intracoastal Waterway.
1900 SE 15th St. Tel: (954) 763 2777. Open: daily 11.30am–10pm.

Mark's Las Olas ★★★
Sophisticated Florida fusion cuisine using the freshest of ingredients. Dinner reservations required.
1032 E Las Olas Blvd. Tel: (954) 463 1000. Open: Sun–Thur 6.30–10pm, Fri & Sat 6.30–11pm.

ENTERTAINMENT
Broward Center for the Performing Arts
Fort Lauderdale's showpiece arts centre specialising in theatre and opera.
Riverwalk Entertainment District, 201 SW Fifth Avenue. Tel: (954) 462 0222; www.browardcenter.org

O'Hara's Jazz and Blues Café
A decent menu of seafood, sandwiches and bar snacks with live jazz, funk and blues nightly; tables inside and on the sidewalk.
722 E Las Olas Blvd. Tel: (954) 524 1764. Open: daily 11am–late.

Carrie B
Sightseeing tours aboard a stately paddleboat with an a/c lounge and an open deck upstairs.
440 North New
River Drive E.
Tel: (954) 768 9920;
www.carriebcruises.com

Sea Experience
Glass-bottom boat tours with snorkelling, as well as scuba diving trips and instruction.
801 Seabreeze Blvd.
Tel: (954) 770 3483.

KEY WEST
SPORTS AND LEISURE
Pepe's ★/★★
Popular local diner with excellent barbecues.
806 Caroline St.
Tel: (305) 294 7192.
Open: daily 7.30am–10.30pm.

Rick's Blue Heaven ★★
Hemingway once refereed boxing matches here. West Indian foods served.
129 Thomas St.
Tel: (305) 296 8666.
Open: daily 8am–10.30pm.

SPORTS AND LEISURE
Fury Water Adventures
A glass-bottom catamaran offering reef viewing plus boat cruises, snorkelling and parasailing. Trips leave from various Key West locations.
Tel: (305) 294 8899;
www.furycat.com

Lazy Dog Adventures
Gentle kayak tours through the Key West backwaters with guides pointing out the birds, fish and sealife.
Hurricane Hole
Marina, Key West.
Tel: (305) 295 9898.

ANTIGUA
EATING AND DRINKING
Hemingway's ★★
A lovely setting in a colonial-era building serving fresh, tasty Caribbean food.
St Mary's St, St John's.
Tel: (268) 462 276.
Open: Mon–Sat
8.30am–11pm,
closed Sun.

SPORTS AND LEISURE
Ultramarine
Guided dives and PADI certification.
Sunsail Club Colonna,
Hodges Bay.
Tel: 463 3483;
www.
ultramarinecaribbean.com

Wadadli Cats
Coastal cruises (including island circumnavigation) with snorkelling, lunch and an open bar. Pickups from several west coast beaches.
Tel: (268) 462 4792;
www.wadadlicats.com

ARUBA
EATING AND DRINKING
Iguana Joe's ★★
Popular place serving tasty, reliable Mexican food.
Royal Plaza Mall,
Oranjestad.
Tel: (297) 583 9373.
Open: Mon–Sat
11am–midnight, Sun
5pm–midnight.

SPORTS AND LEISURE
Jolly Pirates
Cruises aboard 'pirate'-type sailing ships with snorkelling and a rope swing off the deck; great for kids as well as adults. Open bar throughout.
Tel: (297) 586 8107;
www.jolly-pirates.com

Rancho Notorious
Horseback rides to a wildlife lagoon, sand dunes or to a coastal

pool, plus guided mountain biking and ATV (quad bike) tours.
Boroncana, Noord.
Tel: (297) 5860 508;
www.
ranchonotorious.com

Red Sail Sports
All-round watery experts, with scuba diving (including diving for kids) as well as catamaran trips, watersports (from banana boats to jet skis), deep sea fishing and various land tours, too, including open-topped jeep safaris.
Tel: (297) 586 1603;
www.redsailaruba.com

BAHAMAS
EATING AND DRINKING
Café Matisse ★★
Laid-back but elegant bistro serving delicious seafood and pasta.
Bank Lane, Nassau,
New Providence.
Tel: (242) 356 7012.
Open: Tue–Sat noon–3pm
& 6–10pm.

Pub at Port Lucaya ★★
Unpretentious place with everything from goats' cheese salad to shepherd's pie.

Port Lucaya, Freeport,
Grand Bahama.
Tel: (242) 373 8450.
Open: daily 11am–11pm.

SPORTS AND LEISURE
Golf courses
Cable Beach,
Grand Bahama
(7040 yards, par 72);
tel: (242) 327 6000;
www.
crystalpalacevacations.com
One and Only
Ocean Club, Paradise
Island, Grand Bahama
(6,805 yards, par 72);
tel: (242) 363 2501;
www.
oneandonlyresorts.com
Blue Shark Golf Club,
New Providence
(6,707 yards, par 72);
tel: (242) 362 4546;
www.bluesharkgolf.com

Chubasco charters
Sport fishing in deep waters for shark, blue Marlin, white marlin, sailfish, yellowfin and blackfin tuna, mahi-mahi ('dolphin') and wahoo.
Tel: (242) 324 3474;
www.
chubascocharters.com

UNEXSO
Scuba diving and swimming with dolphins.

Freeport, Grand Bahama.
Tel: (242) 373 1244;
www.unexso.com

BARBADOS
EATING AND DRINKING
Waterfront Café ★★
Excellent Caribbean cuisine and a pleasant setting on the Careenage.
Bridgetown Marina,
The Careenage.
Tel: (246) 427 0093.
Open: 10am–11pm
Mon–Sat, closed Sun.

Atlantis Hotel ★★/★★★
Excellent luncheon buffet with ocean views. Convenient for Andromeda Gardens.
Bathsheba, St Joseph.
Tel: (246) 433 9445.
Open: daily 8am–10pm.

SPORTS AND LEISURE
Golf courses
Sandy Lane, St James
(7,060 yards, par 72; and 3,345 yards, par 36)
tel: (246) 444 2000;
www.sandylane.com.
Barbados Golf Club
(6,805 yards, par 72;
tel (246) 428 8463;
www.
barbadosgolfclub.com

El Tigre
Catamaran tours with lunch, open bar,

snorkelling and a beach stop.
Tel: (246) 417 7245;
www.eltigrecruises.com

BERMUDA
EATING AND DRINKING
Carriage House ★★/★★★
International and local cuisine at the attractively restored wharf complex.
Somers Wharf, Water St, St George's.
Tel: (441) 297 1270.
Open: daily 11.30am–3pm & 5.30–9.30pm.

SPORTS AND LEISURE
Golf courses
Port Royal, 5 Port Royal Drive, Southampton (6,842 yards, par 71);
tel: (441) 234 0974;
www.portroyalgolf.bm
Mid-Ocean Club, Tucker's Town (6547 yards, par 71);
tel: (441) 293 0330;
www. themidoceanclubbermuda. com
Fairmont Southampton, 101 South Shore Road, Southampton (2,684 yards, par 54);
tel: (441) 238 8000;
www.fairmont.com/ southampton

Smatt's
Mountain bike and scooter rental – ideal for exploring the Bermuda Railway Trail. Several locations islandwide.
74 Pitt's Bay Road, Hamilton.
Tel: (441) 295 1180;
www.smattscyclelivery.com
Blue Water Diving and Watersports
Scuba dives and certification plus kayak tours with snorkelling, underwater scooter tours and sunfish sailboat rental. Two island locations.
Elbow Beach.
Tel: (441) 232 2909;
Somerset Bridge.
Tel: (441) 234 1034;
www.divebermuda.com

CAYMAN ISLANDS
EATING AND DRINKING
Coconut Joe's ★★
Busy, lively bar and restaurant offering everything from rum-laced ribs to fajitas.
West Bay Rd, Grand Cayman. Tel: (345) 943 5367. Open: daily 7am–midnight.
The Wharf ★★★
Seafood, continental and Caribbean dishes and an

attractive waterside setting.
West Bay Rd, Seven Mile Beach, Grand Cayman.
Tel: (345) 949 2231.
Open: daily 6–10pm.

CURAÇAO
EATING AND DRINKING
Iguana Cafe ★★
Inexpensive place, perfect for watching the ships go by as you eat. Seafood and Dutch specialities.
Handelskade, Purida, Willemstad.
Tel: (5999) 461 9866.
Open: Mon–Sat 11am–10.30pm.
Gouveneur de Rouville ★★/★★★
Set in a handsome former governor's residence overlooking the water, with a varied menu that includes some Dutch dishes.
De Rouvilleweg 9, Otrabanda Waterfront, Willemstad.
Tel: (5999) 462 5999.
Open: daily 9am–11pm.

SPORTS AND LEISURE
Ocean Encounters
The largest scuba diving operation on the island, with several branches. Guided dives available.

*Bapor Kibra, Willemstad.
Tel: (5999) 461 8131;
www.oceanencounters.com.*
Yellow Jeep Safaris
These open-topped jeeps
are the perfect way to
explore the island's north
shore or national park.
Pickups from the port.
*Tel: (5999) 462 6262;
www.jeep-safaris.com*

DOMINICA
EATING AND DRINKING
**Papillote Wilderness
Retreat ★★/★★★**
Flying-fish sandwiches,
breadfruit balls and
salads on the shaded
terrace overlooking the
gardens.

*Trafalgar Falls, Roseau.
Tel: (767) 448 2287.
Open: daily 8am–1.30pm.*

SPORTS AND LEISURE
Wacky Rollers
A host of adventurous
activities, from a treetop
adventure park of
traverses and swings to
jeep tours, river tubing
and kayaking.
*Front St, Roseau.
Tel: (767) 440 4386;
www.wackyrollers.com*
Irie Safari
Guided snorkelling tours
in the famously bubbly
waters of Champagne
Beach.
Tel: (767) 440 5085.

Nature Island Dive
Scuba diving, snorkelling
and kayak tours.
*Soufrière.
Tel: (767) 449 8181;
www.natureislanddive.com*

GRENADA
EATING AND DRINKING
The Aquarium ★★/★★★
Beautiful setting on the
sand, and a menu that
ranges from callaloo
cannelloni to ginger-
glazed lobster.
*Pink Gin Beach. Tel:
(473) 444 1410. Open:
Tue–Sun 11am–11pm.*
The Nutmeg ★★/★★★
A great place for a
snack or full meal.

Grand Cayman's Seven Mile Beach

The Lambi (conch) is well done.

The Carenage,
St George's.
Tel: (473) 440 2539.
Open: Mon–Sat
8am–10pm.

SPORTS AND LEISURE
Aquanauts

The island's best dive shop, with multilingual instructors/guides, and two branches.

True Blue Resort,
True Blue Bay.
Tel: (473) 439 2500;
Grand Anse Beach
(473) 444 1126; www.
aquanautsgrenada.com

Spice Kayaking

Eco-oriented guided kayak tours around mangroves, with swimming and snorkelling.

Allamanda Beach Resort,
Grand Anse.
Tel: (473) 440 3678;
www.spicekayaking.com

GUADELOUPE
EATING AND DRINKING
Caraïbes Café ★★

Classic French café with excellent prix-fixe set menus and great coffee.

Malendure Plage,
Basse-Terre.

Tel: (590) 98 70 34.
Open: daily noon–3.30pm
& 11am–4pm.

Le Karacoli ★★

Great French-Creole food served on the terrace at Grande Anse Beach.

Deshaies, Basse-Terre.
Tel: (590) 28 41 17.
Open: daily
noon–2.30pm.

SPORTS AND LEISURE
Les Heures Saintes

The island's largest scuba outfit, with guided dives in the Cousteau Underwater Park; whale- and dolphin-watching trips in the winter season, too.

Rocher de Malendure,
Bouillante, Basse-Terre.
Tel: (0590) 98 86 63;
www.plongee-
guadeloupe.com

Paradox Croisieres

Catamaran trips to Marie-Galante and Petit-Terre islands, with snorkelling included.

Marina Saint-François.
Tel: (590) 88 41 73.

JAMAICA
EATING AND DRINKING
Pork Pit ★

Spicy Jamaican pork, chicken, fish or sausage

jerk cooked on a bed of coals.

27 Gloucester Ave,
Montego Bay.
Tel: (876) 940 3008.
Open: daily
11am–10.30pm.

Toscanini ★★★

Beautiful setting on the porch of an old Gingerbread-designed house, and authentic Italian cooking using the best of local ingredients.

Harmony Hall, Ocho Rios.
Tel: (876) 975 4885.
Open: Tue–Sat noon–2pm
& 7–10.30pm.

SPORTS AND LEISURE
Golf courses

Half Moon, Rose Hall (7119 yards, par 72); *tel: (876) 953 2560; www.halfmoongolf.com* White Witch, Ritz Carlton Hotel, Rose Hall (6,859 yards, par 71); *tel: (876) 953 2800; www.ritzcarlton.com* Cinnamon Hill, Rose Hall Resort, Rose Hall (par 6,637, par 71); *tel: (876) 953 2984; www.rosehallresort.com* Breezes Runaway Bay (5,389 yards, par 72); *tel: (876) 973 7319.*

andals Golf and
Country Club, Ocho Rios
6,502 yards, par 71);
el: (876) 975 0119;
www.sandals.com/golf

Chukka Adventures
The island's leading soft
adventure operator with
several bases across the
island offering zipline
canopy tours, open-
topped jeep safaris, river
tubing, ATV tours,
horseback ride'n'swim,
dinghy ocean safaris,
dune-buggy riding and
dog sledding.
Tel: (876) 953 6699;
www.chukkacaribbean.com

Scuba Jamaica
Scuba operator with
branches in all the
island's resorts.
Tel: (876) 381 1113;
www.scuba-jamaica.com

MARTINIQUE

EATING AND DRINKING
Le Marie-Sainte ★★
Excellent Creole food,
and a good formula set
menu.
160 rue Victor Hugo,
Fort de France.
Tel: (0596) 71 54 16.
Open: Tues–Fri 9am–
3pm, Sat 8am–3pm.
La Belle Epoque ★★★
Upscale place serving

classic French cuisine
from foic gras to fish in
lemon sauce; and a
good-value prix-fixe set
lunch menu.
97 Route de Didier,
Fort-de-France.
Tel: (0596) 64 41 19.
Open: Mon–Sat 11am–
3pm & 6.30–10pm, closed
for lunch Mon & Sat.

SPORTS AND LEISURE
**Martinique Golf and
Country Club**
Les Trois-Ilets
(6,640 yards, par 71)
tel: (0596) 68 32 81;
www.golfmartinique.com
Ranch Jack
Horseriding trails
through the countryside,
as well as on the beaches
and into the sea.
Morne Habitué,
Trois Ilets.
Tel: (0596) 68 37 69; www.
martinique-equitation.fr

PUERTO RICO

ACCOMMODATION
Gallery Inn ★★
Beautifully decorated
boutique hotel in a
stunning old building
with greenery-swathed
courtyards, a pool and a
'wine terrace' with
sweeping sea views and

lovely public areas.
204–206 Norzagaray,
Old San Juan.
Tel: (787) 722 1808;
www.thegalleryinn.com
Hotel El Convento
★★/★★★
A lovely upscale hotel
occupying a former
convent with elegant
rooms overlooking the
sea and excellent
facilities.
100 Cristo Street,
Old San Juan.
Tel: (787) 723 9020;
www.elconvento.com

EATING AND DRINKING
El Picoteo ★★
Set inside the grand
Hotel El Convento,
and offering 100-plus
tapas dishes as well as
more substantial
Spanish food.
Hotel El Convento, Calle
Cristo 100, Old San Juan.
Tel: (787) 723 9202.
Open: Tue–Sun 11am–
11pm.
The Parrot Club ★★/★★★
A San Juan institution
serving great local food
with an international
twist and offering live
jazz some evenings.
Calle Fortaleza 363,
Old San Juan.

Tel. (787) 725 7370.
Open: Mon–Fri
11.30am–3pm, Sat & Sun
noon–4pm.

ENTERTAINMENT
Lights and Shadows
Puerto Rico's history
brought to life by way of
a sound, light and laser
show in the atmospheric
setting of the Castillo San
Cristóbal.
*Tel: (787) 964 1011; www.
lightsandshadowspr.com*
Carli Café ★★
In the heart of Old San
Juan, adjacent to the
cruise ship piers, with a
varied and excellent
menu and live jazz
nightly from Monday to
Saturday.
*Plazoleta Rafael Carrion,
Banco Popular Building,
corner of Recinto Sur and
San Justo streets.
Tel: (787) 725 4927; www.
carlicafeconcierto.com.
Open: Mon–Sat
9am–late.*
Nuyorican Café ★★
Busy bar celebrating all
things salsa with regular
live music and other
entertainment, and a
basic menu of pizza and
the like.
Calle San Francisco 312,

entrance on Callejón
de Capilla.
*Tel: (787) 977 1276;
www.nuyoricancafepr.com*

SPORTS AND LEISURE
Kayaking Puerto Rico
A host of fun-filled
kayak expeditions
from paddles around
the coast to a day-long
adventure including
lunch and a rainforest
hike/waterfall swim, or
a night-time paddle in
the bioluminescent
waters of a lagoon off
Fajardo. Pickups
available from San
Juan hotels.
*Tel: (787) 435 1665;
www.
kayakingpuertorico.com*
Mike Benítez Sport Fishing
Half- or full-day charters
on state-of-the-art sports
fishing boats.
*Club Náutico de San Juan.
Tel: (787) 723 2292; www.
mikebenitezfishingpr.com*

ST BARTHÉLEMY
EATING AND DRINKING
Le Tamarin ★★/★★★
Delicious salads and
innovative fish dishes.
*Anse de Grande Saline
(1km/⅔ mile).*

*Tel: (590) 27 72 12.
Open: Tues–Sun noon–
5pm, 7–9pm.*

SPORTS AND LEISURE
Marine Service
Half- and full-day
catamaran cruises with
stops for snorkelling;
plus scuba diving and
jet ski rental.
*Quai du Yacht Club,
Gustavia.
Tel: (590) 27 70 34;
www.st-barths.com/
marine.service*

ST CROIX
EATING AND DRINKING
Harvey's ★★
Creole lunches, from
seafood callaloo to
barbecue. The kitchen
closes when the food
runs out. Terrace dining
and a broad-ranging
menu.
*11b Company St,
Christiansted.
Tel: (340) 773 3433.
Open: Mon–Sat
11am–3pm.*
Blue Moon ★★/★★★
Sidewalk tables and
dining room in an old
Danish arcaded house.
Good New World cuisine.
*17 Strand St, Frederiksted.
Tel: (340) 772 2222.*

Open: Tue–Fri 11.30am–
*pm, Tue–Sat 6–9pm,
*un 11am–2pm.

SPORTS AND LEISURE
Golf courses
Carambola, 72 Estate
River, Kingshill
(6,843 yards, par 72);
*el: (340) 778 5638.
The Buccaneer,
*007 Estate Shoys,
Christiansted
(5,668 yards, par 70);
*el: (340) 773 2100;
*ww.thebuccaneer.com

Dive Experience
Scuba dives and
certification with
discounts for cruise-ship
passengers.
*111 Strand Street,
Christiansted.
Tel: (340) 773 3307;
*ww.divexp.com

ST KITTS AND NEVIS

EATING AND DRINKING
Fisherman's
Wharf ★★/★★★
Waterside setting on a
pier with good seafood
at the nightly buffet.
*Basseterre, St Kitts.
Tel: (869) 465 2754.
Open: daily 6.30–11pm.
Sunshine's ★★/★★★
Great little beach
bar with simple

seafood and killer rum
cocktails.
*Pinney's Beach, Nevis.
Tel: (869) 469 5817.
Open: daily 9am–11pm.

SPORTS AND LEISURE
Golf Clubs
Royal St Kitts,
Frigate Bay, St Kitts
(6,900 yards, par 71);
*tel: (869) 466 2700; www.
royalstkittsgolfclub.com
Four Seasons,
Pinney's Beach, Nevis
(6766 yards, par 72);
*tel: (869) 469 1111; www.
fourseasons.com/nevis

ST LUCIA

EATING AND DRINKING
The Coalpot ★★/★★★
Busy, semi open-air place
overlooking the marina
and serving great
seafood.
*Vigie Marina.
Tel: (758) 452 5566.
Open: Mon–Fri
noon–3pm & 5–11pm,
Sat 5–11pm.
Razmataz ★★/★★★
This north Indian
restaurant is a welcome
addition to the island
cuisine.
*Reduit Beach Avenue,
Rodney Bay.
Tel: (758) 452 9800.

Open: Wed–Mon
4–11pm.

SPORTS AND LEISURE
St Lucia Golf Club
Cap Estate
(6771 yards, par 71);
*tel: (758) 450 8523;
www.stluciagolf.com
Scuba St Lucia
Full service scuba outfit
with guided diving and
snorkelling in St Lucia's
Marine Park.
*Anse Chastanet.
Tel: (758) 465 8242;
www.scubastlucia.com
Endless Summer
All-day and sunset
catamaran cruises
from the Rodney Bay
area with stops for
swimming and
snorkelling.
Tel: (758) 450 8651;
www.stluciaboattours.com

ST MARTIN/SINT
MAARTEN

EATING AND DRINKING
Taloula Mango's ★★/★★★
Breezy place overlooking
the water with
everything from
burgers to conch
with dumplings, and
live music to
accompany lunch
on weekdays.

St Rose Arcade, Front St,
Philipsburg.
Tel: (599) 542 1645.
Open: daily 11am–late.

La Vie en Rose ★★/★★★

Elaborate dinners in this
1920s style restaurant.
Bld de France at rue de la
République, Marigot.
Tel: (590) 87 54 42.
Open: Mon–Sat
noon–3pm & 6.30–10pm.

SPORTS AND LEISURE

Lee's Deep Sea Fishing

Friendly sport fishing
charter company
attached to a fish
restaurant, where you
can cook and eat your
catch if you so desire.
84 Welfare Road,
Colebay, St. Maarten.
Tel: (599) 544 4233;
www.leesfish.com

Ocean Explorers

Long-established scuba
diving company with a
wide range of courses.
Simpson Bay Beach,
St Maarten.
Tel: (599) 544 5252;
www.stmaartendiving.com

ST THOMAS

EATING AND DRINKING

Gladys' Café ★

Chowders, sandwiches,
burgers and local

dishes served in a
courtyard. Excellent
fruit punch.
Waterfront, at Royal Dale
Mall, Charlotte Amalie.
Tel: (340) 774 6604.
Open: Mon–Sat
8am–2pm.

Agave Terrace ★★/★★★

A sweeping panorama
and superb cuisine
including red snapper
with lobster medallions
and seafood in a host of
sauces.
Point Pleasant Resort,
6600 Estate Smith Bay,
St Thomas.
Tel: (340) 775 4142.
Open: daily 6–10pm.

SPORTS AND LEISURE

**Mahogany Run
Golf Course**

(6.022 yards, par 70)
1 Mahogany Run Road.
Tel: (340) 777 6250;
www.
mahoganyrungolf.com

Snuba of St Thomas

A cross between scuba
diving and snorkelling,
in which you swim
underwater and breathe
via a tube from the
surface.
Coki Beach.
Tel: (340) 693 8063;
www.visnuba.com

ST VINCENT AND THE GRENADINES

EATING AND DRINKING

Frangipani ★★/★★★

Seafood specials and
snacks served on a
delightful, tree-shaded
informal waterfront
terrace.
Port Elizabeth, Bequia.
Tel: (784) 458 3255.
Open: daily 7.30am–10pm

SPORTS AND LEISURE

Dive Bequia

Reliable dive shop close
to all the action in Port
Elizabeth and offering
guided dives and tuition.
Belmont Walkway, Bequia
Tel: (784) 458 3504;
www.bequiadive.com

TORTOLA

EATING AND DRINKING

Pusser's Pub ★★

Full international menu
restaurant upstairs; deli
sandwiches, pizzas and
English pub grub below.
Waterfront Drive,
Road Town.
Tel: (284) 494 2467.
Open: 11am–midnight.

SPORTS AND LEISURE

Caribbean Fly Fishing

Try your hand at
saltwater fly-fishing,

with tarpon the main catch.

Nanny Cay Marina, Tortola.
Tel: (284) 494 4797;
www.caribflyfishing.com

TRINIDAD AND TOBAGO

EATING AND DRINKING

Veni Mangé ★★
Appealing local lunch spot in a colourful old house serving spicy and delicious Trinidadian specialities.
67a Ariapita Ave,
Port of Spain,
Trinidad.
Tel: (868) 624 4597.
Open: Mon–Fri

11am–3pm plus Wed & Fri 7–11pm.

The Blue Crab ★/★★★
A favourite with locals. Serves stuffed crab backs and an array of Creole dishes.
Robinson St,
Scarborough, Tobago.
Tel: (868) 639 2737.
Open: Mon–Fri
11am–3pm.

La Belle Créole ★★★
Terrace restaurant with lovely views over Bacolet Bay and sublime Creole cooking.
Half Moon Blue Hotel,
73 Bacolet St,
Scarborough, Tobago.
Tel: (868) 639 3551.

Open: daily 8am–10.30pm.

SPORTS AND LEISURE

Mount Irvine Bay Golf Club
An award-winning 18-hole course with great views of the sea.
Mount Irvine Bay, Tobago.
Tel: (868) 639 8871;
www.mtirvine.com

Tobago Dive Experience
Scuba diving in the rich waters of Speyside, famous for its drift diving and friendly manta rays.
Manta Lodge,
Speyside, Tobago.
Tel: (868) 660 4888; www.
tobagodiveexperience.com

A fruit boat plying its trade in St Lucia

Index

Acknowledgements

Thomas Cook Publishing wishes to thank the photographers, picture libraries and other organisations, to whom the copyright belongs, for the photographs in this book.

PICTURES COLOUR LIBRARY 1, 44, 100, 107, 109, 135, 141
DREAMSTIME R Goldberg 147, 168, 189, J Gynane 21, K Chen 32, L Trecartin 42, B Howard 59, Slidepix 64, L Weslowski 165, L Neeleman 111, E Riviera 113, Melonesaj 123, V Borilov 153, Alysta 154, C Opstal 161, S Nicholl 175, D McKinney 183
MARY EVANS PICTURE LIBRARY 14, 15, 86, 87
POLLY THOMAS 97, 99, 127
THOMAS COOK OPERATIONS LIMITED 10, 145
WORLD PICTURES/PHOTOSHOT 7, 8
The remaining pictures are held in the AA PHOTO LIBRARY and were taken by DAVID LYONS with the exception of: pages 47, 53, 65, 66, 79, 81, 85, 90, 104, 116, 132, 133, 137, 139, 140, 149, 150, 151, 174 which were taken by Peter Baker; and pages 31, 34, taken by Pete Bennett.

For CAMBRIDGE PUBLISHING MANAGEMENT LTD:
Project editor: Tom Willsher
Typesetter: Trevor Double
Proofreader: Claire Boobbyer
Index: Marie Lorimer

SEND YOUR THOUGHTS TO
BOOKS@THOMASCOOK.COM

We're committed to providing the very best up-to-date information in our travel guides and constantly strive to make them as useful as they can be. You can help us to improve future editions by letting us have your feedback. If you've made a wonderful discovery on your travels that we don't already feature, if you'd like to inform us about recent changes to anything that we do include, or if you simply want to let us know your thoughts about this guidebook and how we can make it even better – we'd love to hear from you.

Send us ideas, discoveries and recommendations today and then look out for your valuable input in the next edition of this title.

Emails to the above address, or letters to traveller guides Series Editor, Thomas Cook Publishing, PO Box 227, Coningsby Road, Peterborough PE3 8SB, UK.

Please don't forget to let us know which title your feedback refers to!